Advance Praise for *Active Peace*

Much has been written about the outward aspects of urgently needed environmental restoration but not enough on the worldview shift and deep inner healing necessary for any lasting change. Scott Brown's new book *Active Peace: A Mindful Path to a Nonviolent World* provides inspiring and useful guidance in this area. In clear, readable prose he helps us understand both the outer and inner context of our collective situation and walks us through the practical, psychological, and spiritual steps toward true, enduring restoration.

—Linda Buzzell, M.A., LMFT, psychotherapist,
and co-editor, *Ecotherapy: Healing with N*

Scott Brown has given us a comprehensive manual fc
and consciously maintaining our relationship with
To be touched by its beautiful narrative and commit
cerning practices offered in its pages is to invite hea
epiphanies that dissolve all illusions of disconnection
the soul in a visceral experience of Interbeing. *Active*
us far beyond restorative justice or restorative act
a restorative way of life. This book is clearly hazard
willingness to settle for separation.

—Carolyn Baker, Ph.D., author of *Love In The Age of Ecological Apocalypse: Cultivating The Relationships We Need To Thrive* and *Collapsing Consciously: Transformative Truths For Turbulent Times*

Too many of us committed to social and environmental justice burn out and become susceptible to toxic emotions such as despair and futility. *Active Peace* responds with a deep exploration of sources for personal growth and resilience. The book offers strong foundations for creating healthy communities and, ultimately, magnificent movements. It is rich in purposeful, humane scholarship and very practical suggestions. 'Top shelf' reading for the life-long activist.

—Charlie Cray, activist and coauthor of *The People's Business:*
oring Democracy

Active Peace is a wise, uplifting, and heart opening book about relationship to self, others, nature, and the world. Scott Brown masterfully presents profound concepts and transformative exercises in a direct, accessible way. His personal and universal stories add warmth and depth. This is a keeper to read, re-read, and apply to our lives!

—Shelley Tanenbaum, Psy.D., Clinical Psychologist
and creator of Intuitive Life Movement®

Scott Brown has written a beautiful and truth seeking book which skillfully weaves together spirituality, restorative justice, ecopsychology, and activism. I highly recommend this book to anyone seeking a new and inspiring model for the necessary union of inner life and outer service to the world. This is the path to our sanity and salvation.

—Jed Swift, M.A., Former Co-Director of the Naropa
University Ecopsychology Graduate Program

Active Peace inspires us all to create a life-affirming society and educates us as to why this is essential for the flourishing of all life.

—Lori Pye, Ph.D, President, Viridis Graduate Institute

Active Peace makes it clear that while transformation is, ultimately, an inside job, the inner is not separate from the outer; in fact, nothing is separate and our survival depends on our full and passionate embrace of this truth. This important book helps us move in that direction in a grounded and resilient way—fully connected to earth, Spirit, ourselves, and other beings. Scott Brown has walked the path and offers wise guidance that will benefit many people and the evolution of humanity and consciousness itself. I welcome and celebrate this book!

—Steve Farrell, Worldwide Coordinating Director, Humanity's Team

One of Scott Brown's strengths is his voice. His voice is very inviting—honest and down to earth. Those who read his book will feel hope rather than despair. If reading a book is a relationship, Scott is a likable author who I trust and want to journey with.

—James Churches, Award-winning author of the satire novel,
Pirates of the Potomac, memoirist, and biographer

ACTIVE PEACE

ACTIVE PEACE

A MINDFUL PATH TO A
NONVIOLENT WORLD

G.Scott Brown

Collins Foundation Press

Published by the Collins Foundation Press
4995 Santa Margarita Lake Road
Santa Margarita, CA 93453
www.CollinsFoundationPress.org

Managing and Production Editor - Cheryl Genet

Cover and book design by Cheryl Genet

Cover photo: *Until You Return* by Earl Wilkerson
Author photo by Samhitta Jones

In text photos by G. Scott Brown and Stephen R. Jones

Includes biographical references

ISBN 978-0-9884382-9-3

Typeset in Adobe Garamond Pro: Garamond is a group of old-style serif typefaces named after Claude Garamont (c. 1480-1561). Adobe Garamond is considered to be among the most readable serif typefaces and has been noted as one of the most eco-friendly fonts when it comes to ink usage.

A Tree Tax of $.25 for each book printed will be donated to: The Canopy Project, planting trees all over the world.

http://earthday.org/campaign/canopyproject

This book is dedicated to the children—whose innocence and vulnerability open my heart and remind me why peacemaking is the great work of our time.

Contents

Expanded Table of Contents

Foreword

"Where I am wounded, make me firm and whole. May all creatures gaze on me with the eye of the friend, may I gaze on all creatures, may we gaze on all with the eye of the friend."
— Yajur Veda (Translation by Sri Aurobindo)

"Not to turn in hate, but to join in love was I born."
— Antigone in "Antigone" by Sophocles

Active Peace is a wise, passionate, finely written contribution to the growing literature on Sacred Activism—the movement now gathering force globally to bring profound spiritual peace, energy, and wisdom together with radical action to help humanity in its extreme crisis go forward with humble power and effective grace.

Scott Brown has brought a wide and rich variety of life experiences to bear on the crucial subject of how to make and live peace in a world ravaged by violence. He was on the frontlines of activism for fifteen years before dedicating his life to learning the ways of peacemaking. He is now a life and relationship coach, a youth mentor, and a trainer grounded in restorative justice, ecopsychology, psychotherapy, mediation, meditation, and wilderness rites of passage work.

As you will see when you read this book, Scott has practiced and modeled the traits and characteristics he's inviting us to invoke in ourselves as we work for a sane and peaceful world: he's unsparingly honest and emotionally open and vulnerable, willing to share the burdens and subtle revelations of his brave heart and his ways of staying infused with hope and energy in a world in turmoil. *Active Peace* is not armchair philosophizing: it is a passionately engaged and pragmatic message from the trenches of a life devoted to service.

Active Peace addresses head-on the most poignant and urgent question of our time: How can we create a nonviolent world? Scott Brown's answers are not naive or facile. He calls us in a way that is both inspired by and grounded in the difficult sacred work of integrating "being" and "doing." The path Scott presents, with its many luminous and potent experiential exercises, invites us into feeling, in the depths of our embodied wisdom, that interrelatedness and interbeing that all the great sages and religious traditions have recognized as the essential truths of reality. When a critical mass of people live in and act from that ultimate truth, when there is authentic peace in the mind and heart, sustained by the hard work of daily practice and enacted in all the regions of life, only then can there be peace on earth.

One of the greatest strengths of *Active Peace* is that Scott Brown doesn't merely present his understanding that the belief in separateness is the root cause of our exploding crisis and much of our personal suffering; he also offers us real ways of restoring ourselves and our societies. These include mindfulness, cultivating deep relationships in our activism work, embodying nonviolence more consistently, healing our shattered connection with the natural world, and a plethora of interpersonal skills and tools. It is clear that he knows them intimately, and knows that over time, and with consistent commitment, they work, and in ways that can transform us into dynamic peacemakers in a violent world.

Thank you, Scott, for this luminous book; may it leap off the shelves into the arms of thousands of readers, hungry and willing to put its timeless, timely truths into practice. The future of our world, and of life itself, hangs in the balance, and there is no time to waste.

Andrew Harvey
Founder and Director of the Institute for Sacred Activism

Preface

On a blustery November day in 2005, I was sitting on a couch next to my wife, minding my own business, when the marriage counselor broke the silence with the one question guaranteed to strike fear in the heart of an unconscious man. She looked at me and asked, "So Scott, what are you feeling right now?" Feeling? Well, I felt like a deer caught in the headlights. I was about as in touch with my feelings as I was the Rings of Saturn. But in that moment, it dawned on me for the very first time that this disconnection from my feelings was worth paying attention to, that it was part of the reason I was headed for divorce. I didn't share that information, I wasn't ready to go that far, but through that small crack in my armor a little light crept in.

Shortly after that session, my wife and I decided to move ahead with divorce. With the collapse of the dream we had shared, I found myself scraping bottom, and in that place of sadness and uncertainty I was finally able to get in touch with the anger and discontentment that had been stewing inside of me for so long. I didn't understand what was happening, but I knew I was bored with being angry and that something needed to change. Like so many others before me, I had to get knocked down by life before I would start to wake up.

The final shove came with a walk on the beach and a question repeated, "What am I passionate about?" I had been working with this question for some time, and on this night, when a vision came to me of Mahatma Gandhi's face smiling down on me, something clicked. With my background in nonviolent action, this visit from Gandhi made perfect sense. I was being called to prepare myself to be of service in the challenging and violent times ahead. I responded with a deep and humble "Yes" to that vision, and that night my course was set. It was time for me to walk the peacemaker's path.

What I quickly learned on this path is the importance of personal transformation as a foundation. I've come to appreciate that Active Peace is, first and foremost, a process of healing my own belief in separateness. Gandhi knew this, and maybe that's why I saw a twinkle in his eye that night on the beach.

I'm so very grateful for the teachers and teachings that have come my way. As I've worked to integrate, distill, and present what I've learned and experienced for the purposes of this book, I have never doubted there was something worth sharing here. I hope you will agree.

Introduction

When I do not think, and only listen, one drop of rain upon the roof is myself.

—Dogen Zenji

There seem to be more and more people embracing the view that nothing less than a major shift in consciousness is needed if we are to survive the environmental, economic, social, political, and moral crises we face. This is often expressed as an evolution of consciousness and a new relationship with the Earth and each other. Unfortunately, the discussion typically ends there, with no suggestions for how to catalyze and cultivate the shift.

Stepping into the territory of root causes and how to most meaningfully respond is the focus of this book. For me, this project is greatly simplified by the understanding that there is a single root cause underlying not only the collective crises confronting us, but also much of our personal suffering. That cause is the illusion of separateness—the belief that we as humans are separate from each other, from other species, from the Earth, and from our spiritual essence.

One of the key consequences of that illusion is the widespread violence that permeates our world. It makes sense doesn't it, that separateness lies at the core of all the wars we wage, the wars we fight against ourselves—our bodies, minds, and souls—against those we love the most, against those we come into contact with in our day-to-day lives, against people in other countries, and against the Earth?

With that understanding in mind, it becomes clear what we are really up against and how we can respond if we really want to address our predicament at the root level. My own exploration of this terrain has led me to four cornerstones for moving beyond separation and violence: mindfulness, nature-based practices, interpersonal skills and tools, and a restorative approach to activism.

Four Cornerstones:
Mindfulness
Nature-based practices
Interpersonal skills and tools
A restorative approach to activism

Mindfulness is the orientation that ties the threads together and creates endless opportunities to experience interrelatedness in our day-to-day lives. Integrating mindfulness into life in this way results in a spiritual practice that improves our personal health and resilience; restores our relationship to nature; adds depth and authenticity to our relationships with other people; and brings more peace, justice, and sanity to the world.

What we are after here, ultimately, is psychological and spiritual development leading to an expanded sense of self. As the sense of who we really are widens, we begin to see through the illusion of separateness simply because it no longer fits reality.

Stepping beyond the limits of ego into our true nature, we find the clarity and compassion that form an organic and unshakable foundation upon which we can build a nonviolent future.

We get there not as a final destination, but as a process. We co-create a better world through how we live our lives each day, through our intentions and choices. A joyful dedication to ongoing growth and maturation is the price of admission.

In my own experience, working with the principles and practices outlined in these pages has moved me from operating on unconscious autopilot with a lot of anger and resentment, to a place of inner peace and empowerment. It's humbling to reflect on the fifteen years I spent as an environmental campaigner—on the press releases I wrote that blamed and shamed the very people I was supposedly trying to influence, on the unconsciousness, insecurity, and self-righteousness that seems to characterize those years.

I feel compassion for that young man who didn't know any better. I recall that there was nobody who took me aside to say, "Look, blaming and shaming people will just make them more defensive. What you really want to do is build a relationship with them. You don't have to like them but you have to respect them as fellow human beings. Here are some things to think about and work on...."

I don't think my experience is all that unique. This inspires me to share some of my story and the key insights that have so dramatically changed my way of being in the world and improved the lives of the people I've worked with.

A Path of Restoration

The peacemaker path—the way of active peace—described in this book is, ultimately, a path of healing and restoration. As I've talked about the importance of restoration over the last several years, it's clear that it's a concept that resonates with a lot of people. In the original Latin, *to restore* means "to make firm again." Many of us have a natural feeling that we could use a little firming up.

In the context of this book, references to restoration are intended to exude a sense of renewal and empowerment; a healing vision for ourselves and the world. To fully grasp the ideas presented in these pages, it's important to be upfront and clear about a key assumption I make.

Running through the book like an unseen source of groundwater feeding a spring is an assumption and belief that we as human beings have a spiritual essence; that we are, ultimately, spiritual beings arising from a great mystery. The words we use to describe that mystery, such as God, the Divine, Great Spirit, or the sacred, are not what matters. What matters is the felt sense of something greater than ourselves. You may not feel it or believe it, or you may think about it very differently, that's fine. It's quite a paradox that something so beyond the personal is, at the same time, so personal. Feel free to attach meanings that make sense to you with all the concepts presented in these pages.

8

The assumption of spiritual essence is provocative in the context of restoration because it assumes that we are already blessed and beautiful and whole just as we are. And one might ask in response, "What is there to restore in that case?"

Whenever a philosophical question like that comes up in this book or elsewhere, I invite you to turn toward your own experience. Do you feel like there is something to restore, some room for improvement in the way you treat yourself and others? Do you have a longing for more peace and ease, more happiness and joy? Do you feel the limitations of a belief that you are separate from other people, other species, and the Earth as a whole? If you answer "yes" to any of these questions, that is your own invitation to restoration calling you. And because you won't get to qualities such as peace and ease and non-separation through force or other acts of will, having some kind of a path to follow can keep you on track.

My own journey on the path of restoration began with the vulnerability that was exposed when my marriage broke apart in 2005. In hitting that low point, my defenses eventually came down and my mind got quiet. In that surrender I saw that something needed to give, needed to change, and that saying "yes" to that process was the key to my future happiness.

Once on the healing path, I got involved in restorative justice, and this is the second reason why the idea of restoration features so prominently in these pages. Restorative justice grows out of deep indigenous roots and it continues to be practiced in many native communities. In the days before courts and prisons, tribal peoples developed sophisticated models of justice grounded in relationship and interrelatedness.

Rupert Ross, a Canadian judge who worked extensively in native communities, wrote a book that captures the spirit of aboriginal community justice. In *Returning to the Teachings*, Ross describes models of justice where the goal is teaching and healing, not punishment.[1] In these community-based processes, all those affected are involved in getting at the root of the problem, which can include patterns of thinking and abuse that go back generations.

According to Ross, the goal of these justice systems is to re-establish harmony and repair relationships at the personal, community, and spiritual levels. It is understood that punishment cannot achieve that. The threat of punishment closes off honest communication just when it is most needed. Punishment will usually create more shame, and it's often shame and low self-esteem that set the stage for the harm in the first place. In this view, it is believed that jail and other forms of intense punishment take already unbalanced people and move them further out of balance.[2]

The beauty and effectiveness of these indigenous models of healing have inspired the development of alternative ways of addressing crime within the mainstream criminal justice system in North America and around the world.

Outside of native communities, what we call restorative justice (RJ) is not practiced in such a holistic way, but there are important similarities. These include the recognition that crime is a violation of people *and* interpersonal relationships and it creates an obligation to repair the harm to the fullest extent possible. The goal is repairing the harm, not punishment, and offenders, victims, support people, law enforcement, and community representatives are all directly involved in the process.

As a restorative justice facilitator and program coordinator I saw how "RJ" put so many of the values I was longing for into practice. I also saw myself in the various "offenders" I was working with and wished I had such a process available to me when I was lost and harming myself and others. I feel lucky to have experienced firsthand the many ways restorative justice contributes to the healing and transformation so needed throughout society.

The restorative vision offers hope and guidance for personal and social transformation. It's a process and a practice. and the goal isn't perfection, but an expanded sense of self—an understanding, not as an intellectual concept, but as a felt experience that we are not separate from anything.

With an expanded sense of self come many capacities that will serve us well in the challenging times ahead. These include the ability to stay open, to see clearly, and to respond to situations with greater intelligence and integrity.

Healing the relationship to self through mindfulness, to the Earth through nature-based practices, to other people through interpersonal skills, and to the world as a whole through a healing approach to activism, are areas of restorative practice with the power to transform consciousness *and* social systems. This walk we are about to share together on the path of active peace aims at nothing less than ending the insanity and violence that pervades our lives and our world.

PART ONE
Mapping the Territory

"We arise from the same source—from the Ground of Being—as part of the great unfolding of the universe. We are not separate from anything that has come before—not our ancestors, not any living thing, not any 'thing.'"

Chapter One

The Inner Context
of Psychlogical Experience

Most people live, whether physically, intellectually or morally, in a very restricted circle of their potential being. They make use of a very small portion of their possible consciousness....We all have reservoirs of life to draw upon, of which we do not dream.

—William James

One starting point for the discussion of restoration is the real world context of our lives. This encompasses our "inner" psychological experience and the "outer" context of society, culture, and environment. Before beginning to map this territory, let's be clear that in actuality, inner and outer, psyche and society, organism and environment, self and other, are not separate—they interpenetrate and co-arise. Still, it can be useful to break things out for discussion purposes.

With each passing day it becomes harder to ignore the unprecedented crises humanity faces. When the question of root causes comes up, many different responses are heard: the self-centeredness of human nature, capitalism, globalization, industrialization, civilization, disconnection from the natural world, the turn away from God, etc. But these are all symptoms. Looking deeply, we find that it is our thinking itself that lies at the root of the crises.

Our thoughts and beliefs also give rise to our personal suffering. This obviously manifests in a variety of ways but often includes a sense of not being good enough, smart enough, good-looking enough, successful enough, or worthy of love. Often there is a deep and persistent sense of insecurity, lack, fear, and anger. So in both the personal and the social realms, it is the mind itself that must be explored as a foundation for restoration.

A Worldview Based on Separateness

Those of us who grew up in mainstream, Western society are products of a worldview based on separateness. A worldview is an individual's and a society's all encompassing view or perception of reality. It forms a guiding narrative that dictates what is valued and noticed and what is not; it is a story that people live by. The individual worldview is unavoidably influenced by the societal worldview, which is shaped over generations by largely unconscious, and therefore unexamined, beliefs, values, and assumptions.

We have been steeped in a view of reality where living systems such as the Earth and the human body are considered machine-like, and only what can be seen and measured is truly valued. In this worldview, humans are considered separate from, and superior to, the Earth and all of nature, and are thus free to manipulate the world at will.

This dominant worldview also separates human beings from each other and from our spiritual essence—a separation that contributes to the systemic violence and injustice that shows itself in many ways, including war, torture, the death penalty, racism, environmental degradation, and ever-increasing levels of economic inequality.

The belief that we are separate from each other, from the Earth and other species, and from spirit is the big lie. It is the ultimate cause of all our suffering.

To fully explore the origins of the dominant Western worldview goes far beyond the scope of this book. What I offer instead is a brief discussion of three areas that can be considered pivotal: the shift from hunting and gathering to agrarian life, the influence of certain Christian beliefs, and the scientific revolution.

The Agrarian Shift

The earliest beginnings of the illusion of separation may very well lie within the gradual shift from hunting and gathering to an agrarian way of life. Just as the first rivulets collecting high on a mountain gather volume and force as they merge and move down slope, so too the shift to agriculture began humbly and slowly built momentum.

The earliest agriculturists of Europe are believed to have maintained their animistic beliefs, Goddess religion, and conscious participation with nature, despite being sedentary and highly sophisticated agriculturally.[3] The early experiments in agrarian life required real intimacy with nature, but also included the manipulation and control of nature.

Over time, the surplus of food and the geographic stability that the growing of crops made possible led to the first cities and city-states. Larger sedentary populations resulted in more manipulation and control of nature, as well as habitat degradation on increasingly large scales. Eventually, 2.5 million years of hunting and gathering as the dominant way of life used by humans and proto-humans to survive, and which demanded an intimate human relationship with wild nature, was replaced by a lifestyle based on the domestication of plants and animals.

The transition from hunting and gathering to agriculture and city-states surely changed the human psyche in fundamental ways. As this shift occurred, the human/nature relationship and the human relationship with reality itself was reoriented. In his groundbreaking book *Nature and Madness*, the philosopher and human ecologist Paul Shepard, hypothesized about these changes. He surmised significant alterations in the human psyche through changes in what people paid attention to, the accumulation of more possessions, and the turn away from unity toward dualism; for example, crop species would be viewed as good and weed species bad, the wild would be distinguished from the tame, the useful from the useless.[4]

Such shifts represent the initial expressions of the belief in separateness. They must be understood in context: we are talking about very gradual changes in emphasis, perception, imagination, relationships, and beliefs. It is not the crops or even the cities themselves, but the consequences for the psyche that are most significant. Surely the root of the class structures, slavery, and warfare associated with the early city-states predates the city-states themselves. There is no conclusive proof, of course, but it can at least be argued that some of the earliest seeds of separation were planted roughly 10,000 years ago with the spread of agriculture throughout the main population centers of the world.[5]

The Influence of Christian Beliefs in Separation

The legacy of Christianity also plays a major role in the belief in separateness. Significant aspects of Christian belief are readily associated with separateness: the human from the Earth and other creatures, spirit from the body, man from woman, Christians from non-Christians.

I want to step carefully here; I'm no Biblical scholar, and like so many others I find tremendous inspiration in the Jesus story and other aspects of Christianity.[6] I appreciate that there are many different orientations within the Christian tradition, but I also know that even as someone who didn't grow up going to church, I've been influenced by its narratives of separation and duality. Heaven and hell as literal realities, the devil as something separate from the psyche, the sins of the flesh, humans having dominion over the Earth, and the notion of "Original Sin"—all of these concepts (and many others) continue to permeate our culture and conditioning.

The consequences of the belief in separateness play out dramatically in this arena: slavery, the Crusades, the Spanish Inquisition, and witch burning are just a few well-known Church-sanctioned activities. And while we don't need to go into detail here, let's do consider the witch hunts a bit more closely.

Harkening back to the Genesis story and humanity's "fall" in the Garden of Eden, who do we find taking the heat? Yes, that would be Eve, and with that indictment, a unique dimension of separation was instilled in the Western worldview and given an air of official legitimacy. From today's vantage point, it seems reasonable to conclude that fear of life and the body led to the placement of women in their own (lesser) category due to their association with life—with nature, birth giving, and the bodily. The female body is, after all, the vehicle for bringing us into the world with all its messiness, ethical dilemmas, pain, and suffering.

There is a clear context within the fundamentalist beliefs of the day that sanctioned and led to the witch hunts—the scapegoating of women as women *and* as practitioners of Earth-based spirituality and healing. The Christians who, in 1486, wrote the Inquisitors handbook, the *Malleus Maleficarum* (*The Hammer of Witches*), explained quite clearly why they believed women were more likely to become witches than men:

> Because the female sex is more concerned with things of the flesh than men; because being formed from a man's rib, they are only "imperfect animals" and "crooked" whereas man belongs to a privileged sex from whose midst Christ emerged.[7]

It is estimated that in Europe between the 15th and 18th centuries, more than 8 million women were killed.[8] But it doesn't end there. From the blame and antipathy toward women, the aversion and separation flows to the Earth herself as the ultimate expression of the life principle. Eco-feminists such as Susan Griffin have illuminated this dark intersection. Griffin opens her book, *The Roaring Inside Her*, with these words:

> He says that woman speaks with nature. That she hears voices from under the earth. That wind blows in her ears and trees whisper to her. That the dead sing through her mouth and the cries of infants are clear to her. But for him the dialogue is over. He says he is not part of this world, that he was set on this world as a stranger. He sets himself apart from woman and nature.

Like me, you may know all too well from your own experience that this legacy of separation continues to be perpetuated by

Christian fundamentalist factions—factions that often seem to hold inordinate political sway. I hope that, like me, you have also experienced the healing message of some of the denominations who are interpreting Christian teachings in a much more holistic and spiritual way. After all, Jesus himself set the bar for serious peacemakers.

The Scientific Revolution

As the year 1610 began to draw to a close, Galileo Galilei struck a decisive blow for the scientific revolution by upturning centuries of belief that the Earth and humans were at the very center of the universe. With his trusty telescope, Galileo conclusively demonstrated that Venus orbited the sun and not the Earth and thereby confirmed the heliocentric planetary system Copernicus had postulated in the early 1500's. Between them they upended an entire cosmology—the understanding of the universe and humanity's place in it.

For the mainstream Christian mind of the day, the displacement of the Earth and humans from the center of the universe meant that transcendence of the earthly realm became even more urgent for the salvation of the human soul. How convenient then, that Galileo's discovery came at a time when the human mind itself was being elevated and celebrated above all else. This was the end of the Renaissance, when Greek rationalism had been rediscovered, and the beginning of the Enlightenment, the Age of Reason. Philosophers and philosopher-scientists such as Francis Bacon, Rene Descartes, Thomas Hobbes, and John Locke were all influential in promoting rationality and empirical knowledge as humanity's ultimate guiding light. But there was one man, more than any other, who set the course of the scientific revolution and stamped his name onto the worldview that dominates Western thought to this day: Sir Isaac Newton.

Isaac Newton (1642–1727) was accomplished in many fields, but it is his *Philosophiae Naturalis Principia Mathematica*, (Mathematical Principles of Natural Philosophy), published in

1687, which has had the most far-reaching impact. In this work, Newton explained the functioning of the universe with mathematical precision. And while the scientific aspects of Newton's thinking continue to impress, there was and continues to be a devastating shadow side as well.

In this *mechanistic* or *Newtonian* worldview, only what can be observed and quantified is considered important. The unseen, interior, subjective, interconnected, holistic, and sacred aspects of reality are left out. With the focus on parts instead of wholes, and the machine-like treatment of the universe, the innate holism and sacredness of the world disappears from consciousness. It has been called the "disenchantment of the world," and it became the foundation upon which modern society was built.

A Life-Denying Worldview

The worldview of the society one is born into, along with the environment, forms the basic context for psychological development. Parents (or other primary care-givers), extended family and friends, teachers and day care personnel, peers, social norms and expectations—all are profoundly influenced by the dominant beliefs of the society at large. The primacy of worldview explains the roots of our own beliefs in separateness and why we have created a society that is so far out of alignment with the natural world and the needs of people; a society that is, in a word, so violent.

Regardless of its cultural and psychological origins, the belief in separateness forms a defining aspect of our psychological inheritance. An old and deeply rooted worldview is transmitted to and through us that assumes humans are separate from each other, from other species, and from the Earth; that the mind is separate from the body, the body and mind separate from God, and spirit separate from anything that matters.

When we deny the wholeness, interrelatedness, and sacred essence of life, we undercut and deny life itself. Acting from a place of separateness, we undermine and withhold some of our most basic human needs, such as safety, belonging, connection, sexual expression, ease, peace, and freedom. Our life energy is itself constrained and denied.

The belief in separateness leads directly to violence. A sense of "otherness" is what paves the way to resentment, hatred and fear, and actions ranging from bad-mouthing to mass murder.

For all the reasons cited above, and because it conveys something of what is at stake if followed to its natural conclusion, the dominant worldview can aptly be considered *life-denying*.

Even into my early forties, I was definitely caught up in life-denying patterns of belief, thinking, and behavior. I wasn't connected to my body or my feelings. I didn't have any conscious practices for cultivating self-awareness and relationships. I didn't appreciate that life is a miracle. All I had was what I assimilated from my culture and society. I felt separate from just about everything. I wasn't fully human and I wasn't fully alive!

One of the most important lessons I have learned is that I can't change anybody else, I can only meet them where they are. I tried to change the fundamental beliefs of a certain family member for decades—it never worked and only led to acrimony. An understanding of the importance of worldview has helped me understand why it is that psychological change has to come from within the individual. This is part of the reason why shame, blame, and fear are ineffective tactics for fundamental social change.

An understanding of the importance of worldview also helps explain why, as more holistic and life-affirming beliefs and values vie to supplant the life-denying values of industrialized society, we find the *systems*—systems such as the educational, legal, and political systems—of society very resistant to change. If the underlying beliefs don't change on a broad-based level, the systems created by those beliefs won't change either.

To fully appreciate what the belief in separateness has wrought, it will be helpful to look in more detail at two of the most basic ways it shows up in our lives: the human/nature split and the human/spirit split.

The Human/Nature Split

A key aspect of our restorative context is the human/nature split—the largely unconscious belief that we are separate from nature. Of course humanity never has been and never will be separate from nature, but we have come to believe that we are, and, consequently, our behaviors and technologies are undermining life on Earth. As the day-to-day functioning of industrial society continues to wreak havoc on the planet, individuals and even organized groups seem nearly powerless to change things in any kind of fundamental way.

The field of ecopsychology delves into this territory and points directly to the human/nature split as the root cause of our degrading and shortsighted treatment of the Earth and other species. While it has roots in indigenous cultures, contemporary ecopsychology has developed over the past couple of decades as some environmentalists and psychologists began to think about the environmental crisis and its relationship to the psyche.

Ecopsychology gives voice to our embeddedness in the Earth and how our health and sanity are intimately tied to the health of the natural world. There are compelling arguments to make that our imaginations, our ability to feel and experience, and our sense of meaning and purpose have all been damaged by the lack of conscious and intimate participation with the Earth.[9] It makes sense, since we are of the Earth from the very beginning, with bodies and minds that developed over millions of years for finely tuned and direct relationship with virtually every aspect of the Earth—with plants and animals, water and wind, soil and seasons.

Given the reciprocal relationship between humans and nature, it follows that there is something pathological in the thinking of

people—and I mean virtually all of us—who allow and perpetuate the degradation of their life-support system. It also follows
that living with such degradation will negatively impact people's
psyches in profound ways.

Having lost much of our conscious connection to the natural
world and our own bodies, it is little wonder that depression,
drug abuse, violence, obesity, attention deficit disorder, excessive
materialism, and many other symptoms of psychological imbal-
ance have arisen on such massive scales. The root meaning of
the word *insane* is "not whole," and this characterizes industrial
society and the psychic splits it perpetuates in a poignant way.

What is most important in the human/nature split is the diminishment in the *relationship* people have with nature—with the
land, with other species, with water and air, with the Earth as a
whole. We've become unconscious of any sense of direct participation with nature even though such participation is happening
with every inhalation and exhalation, every bite of food, every
sip of water, every release of urine and feces. The diminishment
of this relationship has left us so numb that we tend to not even
be conscious of the isolation and loneliness we experience as a
result. It is a form of trauma.

One of the classic symptoms of trauma is *dissociation*, a distanc-
ing of one's self from a very stressful and overwhelming experience. Dissociation functions as a kind of protection mechanism
that favors unconscious numbness over further experience of
the traumatizing situation. In the context of the human/nature
split, dissociation may serve to keep us unaware of our pain
and the depth of our feelings and needs—our longing for connection and intimacy with the natural world—and our love of
life itself. This numbing allows us to continue to participate in
systems and a way of life that causes so much harm.

The psychiatrist Robert Jay Lifton coined the phrase *psychic
numbing* and he noted that, "Within this culture, you could call
the numbing of everyday life a necessary defensive maneuver."[10]

A vicious cycle is in play whereby the separation of the psyche from nature leads to destruction of the natural world, leading to further separation, dissociation, and destruction.

I know from my own experience that even though I have always loved the natural world, I still to this day hold an internalized belief that I'm separate from nature. I notice it when I try to be still and really melt into a place. Even in the most beautiful and peaceful places, I often experience a monkey-like mind and a pull to "do" something other than relax. Even in an earthly paradise, I can feel homeless.

I also know the belief in separateness is in play from the way I treat other beings when I'm operating on autopilot. For example, in the way I think and feel about the butterfly that gets smashed on the windshield of my car. Beautiful, graceful, and the ultimate symbol of transformation, I view butterflies with awe and reverence. But in the end, with an internalized belief in separateness, they are *only* butterflies, and the dead one on my windshield is quickly forgotten.

The shift that I'm trying to cultivate isn't about becoming a fundamentalist and insisting on proper burials for each insect I kill, swearing off driving forever, or "should-ing" myself in any way. Instead, it's a simple but deep longing for a fuller and richer experience of life and more conscious awareness of my inter-relatedness with *everything*. I have felt how being honest about my belief in separateness has opened the door to healing.

The Human/Spirit Split

Another fundamental split created by the life-denying worldview is the human/spirit split. This is the belief that we are separate from our spiritual essence—from the Divine, God, Great Spirit (whatever you want to call it). When that connection is broken, we lose much of our spontaneous, joyful, and intimate communion with life. When only what can be observed and measured is considered real and worthy of attention, our spiritual experience becomes nearly irrelevant, a minor footnote at best.

This may be the most damaging split of them all. While the human/nature split leaves us homeless, the human/spirit split leaves us hopeless. Without a conscious connection to our spiritual essence, we can never know who, or what, we really are, and our growth into an ever expanding sense of maturity will eventually hit a wall.

So what can we really say about the human relationship to spirit? Well, while it may come as a surprise, there actually is enduring wisdom that has been handed down through the generations on this very subject. Known as the *Perennial Philosophy*, this body of knowledge is based on the direct experience of those who have communed most deeply with the divine source of existence. The common themes in the experience of mystics, sages, and certain philosophers, over many generations, have formed a kind of consensus on the spiritual aspects of our humanness.

First used in the 16th century by the Italian philosopher Agostino Steuco, the term Perennial Philosophy was later used by the German mathematician and philosopher Gottfried Leibniz to "designate a universal or shared set of truths that underlie all philosophies and religions."[11] Aldous Huxley dedicated an entire book to it in 1945 called *The Perennial Philosophy*. He later explained its four fundamental doctrines:

> **First**: the phenomenal world of matter and of individualized consciousness—the world of things and animals and [humans] and even gods—is a manifestation of a Divine Ground within which all partial realities have their being, and apart from which they would be nonexistent.

> **Second**: human beings are capable not merely of knowing *about* the Divine Ground by inference; they can also realize its existence by a direct intuition, superior to discursive reasoning. This immediate knowledge unites the knower with that which is known.

> **Third**: [humans] possess a double nature, a phenomenal ego and an eternal Self, which is the…spirit, the spark of divinity within the soul….

Fourth: [a human being's] life on earth has only one end and purpose: to identify [her- or himself] with [the] eternal Self and so to come to unitive knowledge of the Divine Ground.[12]

The Perennial Philosophy points to the experience of waking up and seeing through the illusion of separateness. It encourages us to embrace our spiritual essence as lived experience.

This is transpersonal reality, reality "beyond the personal." It is often referred to as *ultimate, nondual*—meaning literally "not two"—or *absolute reality* and is distinguished from *relative reality*. While relative reality is the world of form—of bodies and matter—absolute reality is the Divine Ground, the Ground of Being, the formless realm of possibility from which we came and to which we will ultimately return.

Absolute reality is beyond all words and concepts. It can't be fully described or known with the intellect because it is beyond all things, including the intellect. In this realm there is no separate entity to do the *knowing*. But, like a fish becoming conscious of the water that surrounds it, we too can experience nondual reality at the level of intuition and experience. When we do, we discover that we are so much more interconnected than we thought we were and that sacredness lies at the very core of what we are.

Bringing focus to the Ground of Being was a game changer for me. It cut through my confusion about "God" and went right to something that just made sense: life and everything in the material world arises from an invisible and mysterious realm of potential. The process is cyclical, seemingly inexhaustible (not even death detracts from it), and its origins lie in something beyond all imagining, something sacred. Embracing this expanded view of reality has allowed me to put myself—my life and my struggles—into perspective; it's the big anchor I throw down when I feel I might capsize.

An appreciation of restoration's psychological context—of worldview and the belief in separateness—helps us understand ourselves and other people better. We can use this awareness to support our own healing, to support others and strengthen our relationships, and to develop more psychologically sophisticated strategies for social change.

Beyond the Belief in Separateness

As strange as it may sound, when I began to understand the implications of the belief in separateness, it came as a relief. It helped me make sense of the violence and insanity of society, as well as so much of my own loneliness and confusion. For years I wanted to know why we seem intent on destroying our life support system and why we kill each other so readily. Now I knew.

I didn't know exactly what to do with that information, but the longing for a greater sense of belonging in the world was irresistible and I couldn't help but move in that direction.

Now, I celebrate having found the teachings I needed and the sense of being in good company as I try to live from the truth of interrelatedness and nonduality. In the Sermon on the Mount, Jesus said, "We are all one." The Buddhist monk and peacemaker, Thich Nhat Hanh, said it plainly too: "We are here to overcome the illusion of separateness." Gandhi understood it as well: "The purpose of life is…to know oneself. We cannot do this unless we identify with all that lives."

A word originating in the Bantu languages of southern Africa expresses interrelatedness and nonduality—*ubuntu*: I am, because you are. And poets such as Rumi, Hafiz, and Kabir made beautiful, timeless art while basking in the divine light beyond the personal:

> *A strange passion is moving in my head.*
> *My heart has become a bird*
> *which searches in the sky.*
> *Every part of me goes in different directions.*
> *Is it really so that the one I love is everywhere?*
> —Rumi[13]

Even science has come to the understanding that the functioning of the universe is based on interpenetrating relationships, energy potentials, and a fluidity of manifestation. Elementary particles themselves have been described as "a set of relationships that reach outward to other things" and "come into being ephemerally through interactions with other energy sources."[14] This has led to a living systems view of reality with an emphasis on interrelatedness and co-creation.

Living Into the Truth of Interbeing

The interrelatedness that is true for particles is true for people too. Thich Nhat Hanh coined the word *interbeing* and I love the way it encompasses the spiritual and practical reality of interrelatedness. We arise from the same source—from the Ground of Being—as part of the great unfolding of the universe. We are not separate from anything that has come before—not our ancestors, not any living thing, not any "thing."

On the most practical levels, we come into the world because of, and in full participation and relationship with, the sun, air, soil, and rain—with all of the elements and processes of the Earth and biosphere. Our being also depends on other beings—on other people and species. Everything from the bacteria in our guts, the decomposers in and of the soil, the insects that provide pollination, the plants and animals we eat, to the phytoplankton, trees, and plants that absorb carbon and create oxygen— we are all in it together, interconnected in a web of relationship and interdependence. Interbeing is a basic truth of our existence.

I have come to appreciate how interbeing includes virtually everything in every moment. Not long ago I was participating in a weeklong training and had several wonderful experiences out in the natural world. One morning, as I stood quietly above a pool in a creek I noticed a large ripple. I looked to see what had caused it and I saw an otter, then two more. I was thrilled to the core and watched them excitedly until they moved out of sight upstream.

One afternoon while at the same training, I saw a hawk fly into a nearby tree and watched until she flew away. I was particularly struck when her wings came into full extension. Later, I felt how the otters and the hawk had become a part of me. I felt the playful, slinky gait of the otters as I walked. I found myself lifting up my arms as I moved about in imitation and reverence of the energy and beauty of the hawk's soaring. I still can't make sense of it with my mind, but somehow their movements and essence found a place to dwell in my soul. I carry them with me to this day.

I noticed the same phenomena as I sat with different people during the training. Sitting with one other person, I realized that all the other people in the room were also present in our relational field. The otters, hawk, trees, and creek were there too. Everything was there in an energetic web of interrelatedness and relationship.

Such experiences have expanded the sense of who, or what, I really am. I've come to realize that my path, with its teachings and practices, has ultimately been a way to live into the truth of interbeing. Concepts alone were never going to override my conditioning—my beliefs and habits of separation. I find that this path is, in a certain way, self-perpetuating. The direct experiences of an expanded sense of self have been so beautiful and enlivening that they keep me open and awake to other experiences. The simple intention to soften the boundaries and align with my true nature feels like purpose enough for this life.

Our lives as humans include rich layers of context. The inner context of psychological experience includes our spiritual essence—the source of the clarity that cuts through all illusions. It also includes the profound wounding resulting from the belief in separateness, which humbles us with the knowing that restoration and peacemaking is ultimately an inside job.

It's a great paradox—that we can be so wounded and have inherent wholeness and divinity at the same time. But as long as we are in these human bodies, the absolute and the relative go together; the formless dances with form. Making one better or higher than the other is just another dualism, another kind of separation.

Knowing this helps keep us grounded. We can feel that support of the Earth with every breath and the countless marvels that surround us—the sublime beauty of birds and their songs, the gracefulness of cats, the peacefulness of deer, the enlivening feel of the sun and wind, the cleansing power of rivers and mountains, the pull of the moon.

Engaging our lives and the world in a more conscious and intimate way, we find the inspiration and resilience we need to continue. This includes building our capacity to face the pain and suffering in the world with courage and compassion.

A Greenpeace Protest in 1990

"We find ourselves living in a pivotal moment. Many crises have converged to show us the insanity in which we are immersed and the consequences of not changing course are becoming ever more clear. The spirit of protest runs high. But it will take more than protest to change things in fundamental ways."

Chapter Two

The Outer Context of Society, Culture, and Environment

It is easy to dodge our responsibilities, but we cannot dodge the consequences of dodging our responsibilities.
—Josiah Charles Stamp

Like a nuclear reaction going out of control, the consequences of the belief in separateness are becoming ever more catastrophic. This is reflected in the growing environmental, social, moral, and political crises we face. It's reflected in the violence we've come to take for granted.

Crisis, however, is but one lens through which we can choose to see the world. Another lens is opportunity, and many inspired people and actions are already laying the groundwork for a life-affirming society. In the following sections we'll explore the view through both of these lenses, as well as the paradox (which we'll discuss in Chapter Three) that holds it all together and consistently eludes black and white thinking.

The Lens of Crisis

The systems we as humans develop to organize our resources and societies originate in the dominant worldview—in our most fundamental collective beliefs and assumptions about the world. Systems such as the educational, legal, and political, referred to earlier, and all the other systems we can name, including the military-industrial complex, the prison system, global capitalism, and the environmental regulatory system, are all products of worldview—of specific beliefs about what's true and what's important.

When the dominant worldview is grounded in assumptions of separateness, when it itself is life-denying, it's not surprising that its associated systems undermine life and health and wholeness at the physical, psychological, economic, and environmental levels.

Furthermore, when the most pressing issues we face are considered together, it's easy to see that they too are systemic in nature. Such issues include the continued threat of nuclear holocaust, population growth, poverty, racism, militarism, dependence on oil and other fossil fuels, and the many facets of the environmental crisis. Climate change, water contamination and shortage, bioaccumulation of toxic chemicals, deforestation and other forms of habitat loss and degradation, species extinction, topsoil depletion, acid rain and ocean acidification, genetically modified seeds and organisms, and the pollution inherent in nuclear technologies—they all come together to threaten life on Earth.

The different threads of crises weave together to reflect the true cost of the life-denying worldview and it is becoming more and more obvious that the issues are interrelated. With this, it is increasingly clear what has to change, and this is nothing less than our individual and collective thinking and fundamental beliefs.

We can acknowledge the benefits of industrial society while still being honest that it is destroying life on Earth. It is not too shocking, once you get used to the idea, that a system so based on separateness cannot hope to last.

Evidence for Industrial Society's Collapse

Let's consider some specific evidence supporting the view that the collapse of industrial society is inevitable and already playing out. Even a short exploration of four topics—dependence on fossil fuels, climate change, damage to the biosphere, and war—reveals something of the depth and seriousness of the predicament we are in.

I fully appreciate that many readers may find their eyes glazing over right about now; that some reason to put the book down and skip over this section may come to mind. It isn't easy to turn and face the "state of the world." But it is essential for the peacemaker to do just that. We don't do it to dwell on the negative; it doesn't mean we live in fear. We face the pain and suffering in the world because we aren't separate from it. We do it as a natural act, as an aspect of our longing for connection and intimacy with life. In the process, we open our hearts and minds and deepen our compassion.

Fossil Fuel Dependence and Climate Change

Burning fossil fuels is causing unprecedented climate change and is subverting the delicate balance that has allowed such a glorious diversity of species, including humans, to thrive on the Earth. Even as climate change becomes increasingly felt through its contribution to superstorms, heat waves, droughts, extended fire seasons and other extreme weather events, the science suggesting that the situation will get worse continues to pile up.

Numerous reports signal alarm over the continued rise of greenhouse gas emissions. A November 2012 report from the World Bank—an agency not known for its environmental activism—found that due to a lack of serious action to reduce greenhouse gas emissions, the world is on track for an average temperature rise of four degrees Celsius before the end of the century.[1]

According to the World Bank report, an *average* rise of 4° C would lead to temperature increases ranging up to 10° higher and "severe disruptions, damage, and dislocation." Such an increase would lead to extreme heat waves and sea-level rise inundating coastal areas in many regions. It would contribute to the loss of species and threaten entire ecosystems, such as coral reefs and large parts of the Amazon rainforest. Global food security would be threatened. Dry regions would get drier, wet regions wetter. All regions would suffer, with the world's poor suffering the most.[2]

The impacts of the pollution associated with the burning of fossil fuels are not limited to climate change. They also include asthma and other respiratory ailments; the accumulation of pollutants such as mercury in water, fish, birds, and mammals; acidification of land and water; and large releases of cancer-causing substances.

Cheap oil is the very basis for Western civilization as we now know it and we find ourselves in the untenable position of sacrificing health, the environment, and long-term security in a vain attempt to sustain industrial growth. But the physics, chemistry, and biology that govern our most basic needs—needs for clean water and air, healthy soil, and a livable climate—are non-negotiable.

Instead of recognizing that we cannot afford to burn even those oil and gas reserves we have ready access to, we are moving in the opposite direction. Instead of moving to wean society off of fossil fuels in a serious way, more and more extreme measures are undertaken to ensure the addiction will continue. Activities such as fracking, mining the Canadian tar sands, building pipelines that span continents, and deep water oil drilling provide ample evidence of this. The lack of a broad conversation on fossil fuel dependence and its implications shows a profound inability on the societal scale to respond to obvious indicators of collapse in the system.

Damage to the Biosphere

Another indicator of industrial society as a short-term experiment is the undermining of the Earth's ecosystem stability and biodiversity. Climate change plays a big role in this but so do other forms of pollution, as well as habitat loss and fragmentation and other forms of human activity. We find ourselves in the midst of the first planetary-level extinction crisis caused exclusively by humans.

The World Wildlife Fund estimates that populations of the world's vertebrate species (mammals, birds, reptiles, amphibians, and fish) have decreased by 50% since 1970 due to human activity. [3] Humans are also driving plant and animal species to extinction much faster than new species can evolve. It is estimated that 150–200 species are going extinct every day, and while extinction is a natural part of the evolutionary process, the current rate is thought to exceed the norm by 100–1,000 times and could reach 10,000 times within two decades. [4]

A relatively high degree of overall ecosystem and climatic stability is the backdrop that has allowed civilization to thrive. As we undermine that stability through habitat loss and fragmentation, species extinction, pollution, climate change, and the unintended consequences of technologies such as geo- and genetic engineering, we move ever deeper into environmental collapse. Even before some of these things started to ramp up, the distinguished anthropologist Roy Rappaport wrote in a 1971 essay:

> It seems to me that the trend toward decreasing ecosystem complexity and stability, rather than the threats of pollution, overpopulation, or even energy famine, is the ultimate ecological problem confronting man [sic]. Also the most difficult to solve, since the solution cannot be reconciled with the values, goals, interests, political and economic institutions prevailing in industrialized and industrializing societies.[5]

If ecosystem stability is too abstract to contemplate meaningfully, we can simplify the threat to life on Earth by focusing on just one thing—the way we treat water. The anthropologist, philosopher, and writer Loren Eiseley famously said, "If there is magic on this planet, it is contained in water." At one temperature range it's solid ice, at another it's liquid water, and at yet another it's airborne vapor. Life giving, powerful, beautiful, and comprising approximately 60% of the human body, if water isn't sacred then nothing is.

Water pollution is one of humanity's most serious violations of what we might call *natural law*—the nonnegotiable chemistry and physics that govern the health and wellbeing of life on Earth. The shortsighted way we use and pollute groundwater, surface water, and the oceans epitomizes the way industrial society acts against life itself and the truth of interrelatedness and interbeing.

The water pollution associated with things like mining, oil drilling, and nuclear power has consequences. Laying oil and gas pipelines along and across rivers has consequences. As this book goes to press, radioactive water from the Fukushima nuclear power plant in Japan continues to leak into the Pacific Ocean and has been doing so since March 2011. I could include so many things in a list like this—the Exxon Valdez oil spill and the British Petroleum disaster in the Gulf of Mexico—but the basic point I'm wanting to make is that violating natural law leads in one direction only and the sign on that road reads, "Warning, collapse ahead."

War and the Culture of Violence

The belief in separateness is deadly, and the belief that we are separate and somehow above nature is a profound expression of this. It can be argued, however, that at least some aspects of industrial society's abuse of nature is unconscious—that we are so disconnected from the Earth and other species that we don't realize what we are doing. The violence we all too frequently inflict on other people and countries, on the other hand, is done quite consciously—with sophisticated planning and budgeting. War, and our intentional preparation for it, demonstrates the twisting of the mind caused by the world-view of separateness.

War, especially war in the nuclear age, cannot be reconciled with our long-term survival. Our survival depends on a shift toward values that prioritize and uphold peace, justice, and environmental sanity. Martin Luther King, Jr. emphasized the need for a revolution of values in his 1967 *Beyond Vietnam* speech:

> A true revolution of values will lay hand on the world order and say of war, 'This way of settling differences is not just.' This business of burning human beings with napalm, of filling our nation's homes with orphans and widows, of injecting poisonous drugs of hate into the veins of peoples normally humane, of sending men home from dark and bloody battlefields physically handicapped and psychologically deranged, cannot be reconciled with wisdom, justice, and love. A nation that continues year after year to

spend more money on military defense than on programs of social uplift is approaching spiritual death.

Dr. King understood that war was a systemic problem. He understood that war and racism, poverty and inequality, were symptoms of sickness. He also understood that, ultimately, spiritual death cannot be separated from physical death, that once the soul is lost, total destruction is inevitable.

I once had the pleasure of hearing a talk by Claude AnShin Thomas, a Vietnam war veteran turned Buddhist peacemaker. He said something that has stuck with me for years. He said war and violence are an expression of our collective suffering. This statement still resonates with me and suggests the deep healing needed to save ourselves.

As the starkest and darkest manifestation of the belief in separateness, I've come to believe that violence is itself the core crisis we face.

Dependence on fossil fuels, climate change, damage to the biosphere, and the perpetuation of war and violence are just some of the indicators of the collapse of industrial society as we know it. When asked on the news program *Democracy Now!* what he thought needed to change about the dominant economic system, the Chilean economist and Right Livelihood award winner Manfred Max-Neef replied, "almost everything." He pointed out that the fundamental flaw lies in putting short-term economic interests above life and the air, water, and soil that sustains life. He concluded that the economic system "is poisonous, dramatically poisonous" and that its demise is inevitable.[6]

The collapse of industrial society is a systems-level predicament loaded with uncertainty and requiring many layers of response. Understanding the role that the belief in separateness plays can focus our attention on root causes and the foundations necessary for creating nonviolent, life-affirming alternatives.

The Lens of Opportunity (The Great Turning)

Danger itself fosters the rescuing power.
— Friedrich Hölderlin

The crisis we face is the wake up call, the planetary and social feedback telling us that we will either change or perish. The good news is that every crisis comes paired with opportunity in equal measure. This seems a natural feature of the paradoxical nature of the universe, the balancing of energies—the light and the dark, the male and female, the warmth of summer and the cold of winter, life and death. The importance of understanding and balancing seemingly opposed energies has been observed by spiritual and philosophical traditions since ancient times. It is the Tao, the way of things, exquisitely captured in Lao-tzu's timeless classic, the *Tao Te Ching*:

> *As it acts in the world, the Tao*
> *is like the bending of a bow.*
> *The top is bent downward;*
> *the bottom is bent up.*
> *It adjusts excess and deficiency*
> *so that there is perfect balance.*
> *It takes from what is too much*
> *and gives to what isn't enough.*[7]

Seeing the opportunity that goes hand in hand with the crisis is vital. Seeing only injustice and devastation poisons the mind with bottomless despair and undermines the ability to act with clarity and wisdom. Seeing only crisis puts us out of balance and makes it easy to play the victim role—equal parts disempowerment and self-righteousness.

The full opportunity before us is to create a nonviolent world. We'll do that through cultivating a life-affirming worldview and building life-affirming structures and systems—ways to be and work together that are cooperative and mutually enhancing.

The shift from a life-denying society to a life-enhancing society has been called the "Great Turning" (Joanna Macy and David Korten) and the "Great Work" of our time (Thomas Berry). If we are to survive, we must turn toward a new era in which we heal ourselves of the belief in separateness and restore our relationships to each other, to the Earth and other species, and to spirit.

We are beckoned toward more meaningful and authentic lives, to embrace holistic ways of thinking and abide with more grace and dignity within the communities and ecosystems we inhabit. On the way we will find fertile ground for realizing who we really are and what we really need.

We find ourselves living in a pivotal moment. Many crises have converged to show us the insanity in which we are immersed and the consequences of not changing course are becoming ever more clear. The spirit of protest runs high. But it will take more than protest to change things in fundamental ways.

I'm reminded of a slogan that was popular at protests in my campaigner days: "What Part of NO Don't You Understand!" I still like that slogan, and while a clear "No" is often a great start, fundamental systems' change has to be built on "Yes." "Yes" to a vision of a better way. "Yes" to personal transformation. "Yes" to treating everyone with respect and dignity. "Yes" to co-creation and collaboration. "Yes" to nonviolence. I now like to envision signs more along the lines of "Join Us in Saying YES To LIFE!"

When we understand that our collective outer reality (society and culture) is a manifestation of our collective inner reality (our thoughts and beliefs), we have the key insight into how the "Great Turning" can come about. That societies change in response to evolving worldviews is obvious enough and much progress has been made. Quick fixes at this level remain elusive, however, and I have none to offer.

What I *do offer* is the understanding that it's essential to our survival to know our context and the fundamental nature of our basic beliefs and assumptions; that violence itself, springing from the belief in separateness, is the primary threat we face; and that this view places responsibility right where it can do the most good: within each and every one of us.

"Freedom and choice—you get to choose your path. In a very real way, the more beautiful and peaceful world you long for is already here."

Chapter Three

Growing Up Together

You can only be young once. But you can always be immature.
—Dave Barry

The scale of the challenges and opportunities before us make it clear why it is so important to expand the sense of who and what we really are. If we are to cultivate a more conscious communion with each other and the natural world, it will take more than positive thinking and sweet dreams.

Paying attention to our inner, psychological context, we come to appreciate the depth of the wound caused by the belief in separateness. Paying attention to our outer context of culture, environment, and society, we face the scale of the task of creating a nonviolent world. And throughout it all, there is our spiritual essence and the gift of human consciousness to steady us and give us courage.

Our culture's profound lack of appreciation for lifelong psychospiritual development is a serious handicap that comes with the life-denying worldview. This is, perhaps, our main obstacle, but thankfully there are teachings and resources directing us toward more mature paths. The Perennial Philosophy, discussed in Chapter One, which helps us understand that the main purpose of our lives is to know our spiritual essence, is an example of just such a resource.

The belief in separateness is a symptom and sign of personal and collective immaturity. A path that continually expands the sense of self beyond the limits of ego, on the other hand, is a mature and worthy path.

Not all cultures are as psychologically and spiritually disconnected as our own. Indigenous cultures typically approach psycho-spiritual development and maturation in a much more conscious way through ritual, ceremony, and wisdom teachings. These include rites of passage and initiations that work at the level of psyche and spirit and alter the worldview itself. According to Malidoma Somé of the Dagara tribe of Burkina Faso in West Africa:

> Growth itself makes one forget who one is. So initiation is something that is designed to help one remember one's origin and the very purpose of one's occurrence on this side of reality—that is to say, why one was born….So a person who is not initiated is considered a child, no matter how old that person is, because that person will not be able to recall his or her purpose. Without initiation, the bridge between youth and adulthood can never be crossed…"[1]

Rites of passage are scary and push us outside of our comfort zones. They invoke the death that is required for life to continue. The initiate dies to the ways of adolescence in order to enter fully into adulthood. Conscious, intentional rites of passage are a journey into the darkness of the psyche, the shadow, the night; they touch into deep fear and the ability to survive that fear. They push people beyond the confines of the personal and into the transpersonal. In that stripped down, vulnerable place, a vision may be received that will help guide the person in a new role as an adult.

Many indigenous cultures understand that, in a very real way, life depends on such initiations; they are the bedrock that has sustained them for millennia. Communities everywhere need the unique visions and wisdom, need the energy and loyalty to the common good that only initiated adults can bring.

How many of us have experienced undertaking our own, largely unconscious, rites of passage where, lacking elders to guide us, we acted out in an attempt to cross the threshold into adulthood? How many people have died due to drugs or alcohol, reckless driving or other forms of violence, and/or a seemingly inconsolable grief? How many have died trying to initiate themselves, doing alone what entire communities used to guide and support?

I know quite well from my own life the sense of being disconnected and dissatisfied, the hunger to know my gifts and to be seen deeply by others. When I was 21, my dad told me I was an angry young man. I was so out of touch with myself I didn't realize how true that was and it would be many years before I would begin to look at that anger and feel initiated into adulthood.

Each experience shapes us. Our wounds give rise to our unique strengths and our sense of purpose. Those with psychic wounds leading to alcoholism can, if they choose it, become exceptional at working with alcoholics. Someone wounded by an abusive parent may become a skillful therapist. People suffering from depression have been some of our most inspired writers and musicians. Somehow, my own experiences led me to engage in the process of making peace with myself, guiding others on their journeys, and being a spokesperson for nonviolence.

Our essence as manifestations of spiritual energy longs to be integrated into our moment-to-moment existence. Engaging that longing as a process and a ripening of consciousness, we grow up together and cultivate the ability to experience our full potential as human beings.

Holding the Paradox

Just when the caterpillar thought the world was over, it became a butterfly.

—Proverb

Our survival now requires us to grow up individually and collectively. The personal and collective rite of passage we both long for and dread awaits us. Our survival depends on our saying "yes" to the call. But we're not meant to do it alone. We can go together, supporting each other along the way.

This is the time to find our "tribes," to find the people and resources that can support us. Since we are not separate from what has come before, we have a vast reservoir of strength and wisdom to draw upon, a deep well of experience and knowing. We are never alone!

When we embrace reality just as it is, with all its paradox, all its challenges and opportunities, the spirit is enlivened and the soul stirred to action. I have far more passion and purpose in my life since I became more able to look unflinchingly at violence and more deeply at beauty. That is an example of holding paradox. And the invitation is out to us all to see the paradoxes we are steeped in, accept them, and let them open our hearts. Paradox is the creative tension that energizes the world.

When we come to know and experience that the world is not black and white, not all sacred light and not all profane darkness, we move toward spiritual maturity. When we understand that, as human beings we have deep wounds *and* incredible capacities to heal ourselves and others, we step more fully into emotional maturity.

The ability to hold paradox allows us to face our predicament head on, with clarity and compassion, and I can think of no greater gift to the world and future generations than that.

The Path of Restoration

*Your task is not to seek love, but merely to seek and find all
the barriers within yourself that you have built against it.*
—Rumi

The crisis we face is severe and plays out on the personal, interpersonal, and collective levels. Restoration is needed because we have all been wounded by a worldview that undermines life itself.

Restoration becomes even more pressing knowing that we can fully expect the social and environmental crises we face to worsen, making it increasingly challenging (and important) for us to work together. There are no easy, pat answers to what lies ahead.

There are, however, psychological and spiritual foundations that can increase our resilience and help us move forward peacefully.

Many teachings tell us that the spiritual path is not about adding anything, but about stripping away what blocks the experience of our own true nature. The wise response is not to try to "fix" ourselves, but to harmonize ourselves with the energies of Earth and spirit, and we do this through practice.

Notice for yourself if and how you feel called to deeper healing and higher purpose. Are you longing to embrace both spirit and the Earth in a stronger way? Do you want to love yourself and others more fully and freely? Are you willing to practice?

In stepping out onto this path, knowing about the Perennial Philosophy and other intellectual concepts can be good support, but the real work lies in each of us bringing it to life in our own unique ways.

The core values of restorative justice help to light the way. These include responsibility, respect, relationship, and repair. We take self-responsibility and ask that of others. We show unconditional respect to ourselves and others. We prioritize relationships and repair them when they are damaged. These are ways of being that align us with our true nature and interbeing. They contribute to our universal needs for connection, intimacy, and trust.

When we actually practice something like prioritizing relationships, we go beyond talk and ideas and live ourselves right smack into the world we want. Through such practice, concepts of a "life-affirming worldview" and a "nonviolent world" lose their abstraction and become a lived reality.

Four Foundations of Active Peace and a Nonviolent World

If the violence resulting from the belief in separateness is the core problem, then cultivating nonviolence is our most important task. Peacemakers do their inner work, but they don't stop there. They put their own lives in the context of *all life*.

If human beings are to survive and live well for generations to come, nonviolence must be brought out into the world in direct and even confrontational ways. Consider Jesus, Gandhi, and Martin Luther King, Jr. They didn't keep truth to themselves. They spoke truth to power and were the most relevant voices of their times because of that. They were also derided, persecuted, and killed as a result. Nonviolence has always been and continues to be the most courageous path imaginable.

The most transformative aspect of nonviolence is the willingness to suffer for a cause greater than oneself. How is that possible without a deep and abiding love that extends beyond the limits of the self?

Connection to God and spiritual essence is what gave Gandhi and his followers, the civil rights marchers, the Freedom Riders, and so many others, the courage to speak out for peace and justice while facing violence and even death.

Transpersonal awareness and experience is the source of the "dangerous unselfishness" of which Martin Luther King Jr. spoke. Because it provides natural clarity and moral consistency, an ever-expanding sense of self beyond the limits of the ego provides the high ground upon which we can march to social transformation. But it must be lived experience—we must know the truth of it deep in our hearts.

How *do* we cultivate such a transformation in ourselves? How *can* we cultivate compassion, empathy, and nonviolence? What *are* the foundations of peace? I believe restorative practices, and commitment to those practices, are the answer.

Mindfulness, nature-based practices, interpersonal skills, and restorative activism are the four cornerstones of restorative practice explored in this book. These cornerstones offer personal and collective healing that provide direct experience of the truth of interrelatedness and interbeing. Each is foundational in its own right and integral in supporting a practical and holistic approach to personal and social transformation.

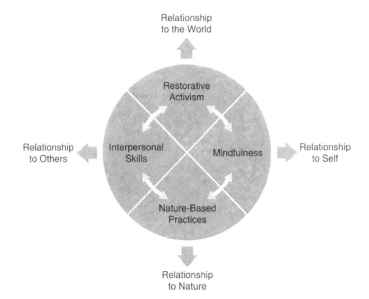

These foundations mark out a path to health and resilience and an active approach to peace. We can follow a path that consistently leads us back into relationship: relationship to self, nature, other people, and the world, as citizens involved in the political life of our communities and country. As we cultivate the capacity to deepen these relationships through specific practices, we develop the awareness we need to live beyond the illusion of separateness and into the truth of interbeing.

It's not a linear process. While we will begin with healing the relationship to self and move around the wheel from there, building a stronger foundation as we go, it's not as if we have to have it all together personally before venturing out into interpersonal relationships or activism. That's obviously not how life works and the soul can't be dictated to in that way.

The transformation that beckons is all about freedom and choice. Notice what's alive for you as you reflect on the foundations presented here. Does increasing your self-awareness and self-acceptance through mindfulness have any juice? Does the idea of deepening your connection to the Earth through nature-based practices speak to you? How about support for your relationships through practicing some concrete skills and tools? Does transforming activism into peacemaking sound compelling?

Freedom and choice—you get to choose your path. In a very real way, the more beautiful and peaceful world you long for is already here. If you can imagine it and feel it in your heart, its energy is here, the seeds already planted. Violence is here too—in your habitual thinking and behavior. The choice is clear: which will you cultivate, which will you feed and water?

PART TWO
The Path of Restoration

"Restoration begins with intention, with the conscious choice and commitment to grow and mature." "Intention focuses awareness and energy, and these are the ingredients that can rewire our brains, shift us out of old patterns, and help us grow into who we want to be."

Chapter Four

Restoring Our Relationship to Self

My mind is like a dangerous neighborhood.
I try to not go there alone.

—Anne Lamont

When I was at one of the Occupy camps shortly after the protests started, Patch Adams came to visit. He is the doctor of love and affordable health care for all—and peaceful revolution too—that Robin Williams made famous in the movie Patch Adams. He was very inspiring in his uncompromising stance toward love. "If it is love that you want and that you are, then just stop holding it back" sums up his message to us that day.

Right after his talk, the group went into its evening general assembly and the love that was spilling out of us just moments before ran screaming from the room. Once again many of us were back in that all too familiar place of wanting to be heard, knowing we are right, and resenting those who disagree with us. Once again we were getting in our own way and disconnecting from our hearts and deepest longings.

While the reasons why the love that overflows one second gets blocked the next is going to vary from person to person, one thing is certain: it's the work of the mind—of thoughts, beliefs, and a limited sense of self.

This is where every war starts, with the beliefs and repetitious patterns of thinking and behavior that perpetuate separation and undermine the heart's inherent wisdom. Personal healing is in no way separate from the healing of society; as always, there is no separation. Please take that in and avoid bypassing this most intimate aspect of restoration, for the sake of yourself, your relationships, and the world.

An evolutionary perspective helps us appreciate much of the mind's defensive, judgmental, and rapid-fire tendencies. Evolutionarily speaking, we are still on the lookout for the crouching tiger waiting to make a meal of us; the mind's basic job is still survival. But like a wild horse trained to be ridden, the mind too can be calmed and gentled.

The work of restoring ourselves is a journey toward ever more self-awareness and self-acceptance. When undertaken with openness and honesty, this journey represents a life-long adventure, with each moment presenting opportunities for curiosity, learning, and change.

Intention as First Step

I have found that beginning all my work—whether it be with myself, individuals, couples, or groups—with a process of conscious intention-setting creates the conditions for transformation. Intention focuses awareness and energy, and these are the ingredients that can rewire our brains, shift us out of old patterns, and help us grow into who we want to be.

Restoration begins with intention, with the conscious choice and commitment to grow and mature. My basic intention revolves around a willingness to understand my mind and take responsibility for my patterns of thinking and behavior, particularly those that undermine my happiness and relationships. Believe me, it wasn't always this way.

Recalling my campaigner days with Greenpeace and other environmental groups, I would say my primary intention back then was to be right, to win every battle and help save the Earth. There is one story I don't relish telling, but it shows this mindset in action, along with some of its consequences.

While I was with the Greenpeace Toxics Campaign, I was invited to participate in a debate with a pulp and paper mill scientist on a local television station in Mobile, Alabama. Greenpeace was campaigning heavily at the time on the use of chlorine and chlorinated compounds in the paper bleaching processes, which were responsible for massive amounts of water pollution.

As the time approached to do the show, which would be aired live, I was well prepared with my arguments about the severity of the pollution this mill and the industry as a whole was causing. I was also well versed in the availability of less-toxic alternatives. Still, I was understandably nervous. Remember, my intention was to be right, win, and save the Earth, all in the span of half an hour.

Our debate started out as those things typically do, with each of us stating and entrenching into our respective positions. Toward the end of the program, however, perhaps realizing that there was no conclusive victory in sight, I exploded. As the scientist was speaking, I shouted at him to "stop lying to people!" I repeated this a few times, and after the host of the show gave a panicked look toward her technicians, our debate was abruptly ended.

Backstage I overheard the *show's* host apologizing to the scientist for my outburst. I was in shock and feeling shame. In holding to my intention to be right and win, I completely lost the high ground. Later, I wondered what the response would be from the allies I had been working with in the Mobile area. The response was a deafening silence. It was a hard lesson.

I'm grateful to now know the power of a conscious, life-affirming intention. My intention is my starting point and also something I come back to when I need help staying on course. If, during that debate, I had held to the simple intention to just tell my truth, I would have done much more for the cause and felt much better afterwards.

Intention shapes how we live by organizing our thoughts and prioritizing our actions. Intention setting is one of the most

powerful capacities we have as humans. This power was experienced in a dramatic way in the extreme conditions of a Nazi
prison camp by the psychiatrist Victor Frankl:

> Every day, every hour, offered the opportunity to make a
> decision, a decision which determined whether you would
> or would not submit to those powers which threatened to
> rob you of your very self, your inner freedom; which deter-
> mined whether or not you would become the plaything of
> circumstance, renouncing freedom and dignity to become
> molded into the form of the typical inmate.[1]

To be restorative, an intention must begin with full ownership
of one's experience and life. In my relationship coaching work,
it's not uncommon that someone will come in with an intention to change someone else. It's the perfect clue that noticing
the thoughts themselves and shifting into self-responsibility is
where this person's inner work begins.

Being willing to set strong, restorative intentions may follow
hitting an extremely low point in life, or experiencing a powerful
teaching or teacher. How we get to this point is important—it
provides the initial incentive to grow. But regardless of what has
come before, what is most important is clarity and commitment
in moving forward.

Restorative Practice
Set an Intention

*Setting a heartfelt intention prior to any activity helps to focus
the mind and assure the time will be well spent. Setting an
intention is a bit like setting a goal but without the focus on a
specific outcome. It is a way to organize our energy and concentration. If there is a goal associated with the activity, we will be
much more likely to meet it if we move toward it with intention
and awareness.*

Right now, before going further with this book, set an intention for yourself related to reading this book.

This book is about changing yourself at the most basic levels of your being. It's also probably not the lightest read in your collection. Why are you reading it? Is there something you want to get out of it?

Is there some longing you have that you hope reading this book might contribute toward? Is there a sense that these practices may contribute something to your life and perhaps the lives of others? There's no right answer to any of these questions—just explore them and see what feels true for you.

Intention setting is a self-awareness practice. What are you aware of right now in regard to reading this book and doing this exercise?

Take your time and feel into an intention for going forward. Don't do it with the mind alone, let your awareness sink down into your heart and your whole being. Again, this book is about change, and change isn't easy. Consider the obstacles that can get in the way. Are you prepared to face these obstacles?

This book is also about self-acceptance. How are you doing with self-acceptance right now? How does this influence your intention for going forward?

Set an intention that is clear and succinct, positive and achievable. Keep it simple.

Take whatever time you need and then speak your intention out loud. Speak it again. Keep your intention alive by making it a part of your aliveness.

Use your intention as a tool for staying focused. Come back to it if your attention and commitment begin to waver.

Self-Awareness and Self-Acceptance

Know thyself so that you may know the universe and the gods.
— Socrates

Working with our minds means cultivating the very basic traits of self-awareness and self-acceptance. With an intention to develop these qualities in ourselves, we take a huge step toward healing ourselves, while also changing the way we relate to others and the world. With an intention to become more self-aware, we sensitize ourselves to what we feel and want, and how we impact others—all on a moment-to-moment basis.

Self-awareness is the very foundation of emotional intelligence. According to the scientist and writer Daniel Goleman, who literally wrote the book on the subject, the fundamentals of emotional intelligence are self-awareness, self-management, social awareness, and the ability to manage relationships.[2] Self-awareness lays the basic building block for functioning smoothly in the world.

This topic hits close to home with me because I know that I lacked any real self-awareness for most of my adult life and this unquestionably impacted every aspect of my life. Now, my on-going commitment to increasing my self-awareness helps keep me open, curious, and (relatively) humble.

Increased self-awareness naturally leads to greater self-understanding. Eventually we begin to not only see, but also to understand our habitual patterns of thinking and behavior. We follow the trail of feeling and emotion to the source. In so doing we learn not only about ourselves, but about the Tao—the universal truth—because we are not separate from it. As the Zen Buddhist master Shunryu Suzuki explained it:

> Each one of us must make [our] own true way, and when we do, that way will express the universal way. This is the mystery. When you understand one thing through and

through, you understand everything. When you try to understand everything, you will not understand anything. The best way is to understand yourself, and then you will understand everything.[3]

As the conscious dedication to increasing self-awareness begins to calm the nervous system, we can tap into the full range of our capacities and wisdom, not just on the rational level but also on the intuitive and transpersonal levels. As we open up more fully to our feelings, emotions, and habitual behaviors—to everything about our experience—we naturally expand our sense of who we are.

Self-awareness also opens the door to self-acceptance. We've all heard that in order to love someone else we must first love ourselves; but what does loving ourselves really mean? I think it boils down to kindness—being kind, accepting, and forgiving toward ourselves. Self-acceptance is essential for our healing because of the shame and self-loathing instilled in so many of us from a very young age.

Far too often, based in part on the wounding that has been handed down through the generations, children are not met with the unconditional love they need by the parents and caregivers they are so completely dependent upon. Too often, the love the parents and caregivers feel gets blocked, and the child gets the message that she/he is not lovable, not good enough—that "something is wrong with me."

Messages such as these become internalized *core beliefs* about ourselves. The most basic core beliefs are preverbal and have to do with the way we are first met by parents, caregivers, and the world at large. In an unconscious and automatic way, we answer questions such as: Is it safe here? Is there enough (food, safety, and love) for me? Can I relax? Later in life other questions arise such as: Is it okay to ask for help? Am I good enough? Is it okay to fully be my unique self?

Unfortunately, the answer to at least some of these questions often turns out to be a resounding "No." And with that no, our life energy is constricted. With that no, separateness becomes a personal experience.

It's little wonder then that a longing for acceptance and love from others comes to direct so much of our lives. And seeking the healing from the outside, we sacrifice self-acceptance and lose much of the power we have to determine our own experience. We become uncomfortable in our own skin.

The main core belief that is mine to work with in this lifetime is that I'm not good enough. I attribute this primarily to my relationship with my father. He was often away and when he was home he was not able to express his love and show his tenderness. Anger, frustration, and criticism overshadowed the love that I know was there. I missed receiving the feeling of unconditional love and blessing—communication from his heart to mine that I was okay just as I was, an appreciation for my uniqueness, a well-wishing on my journey.

The result was insecurity and an internalized belief that I wasn't worthy of love for just being me. That core belief led to a variety of personality traits and behavioral habits—strategies, really—of getting along in the world. I withdrew from anger and avoided conflict. I became very quiet so as to not draw attention to myself. I was afraid to really be seen for fear that the seer would know the depth of my insecurity.

Without ever having done any therapy, when I found myself in a peacemaker training and was asked to tap into my "core wound," I knew just where to go. Right there was my relationship to my father, with all the pent up sadness, rage, and resentment I had kept bottled up for so very long. This was the basic information I needed to begin to understand myself and heal my relationship with my father.

I was in my mid-forties when I began that work, and while I can bemoan the fact that it took so long to find the guides I needed for this self-discovery, I'm grateful to have found them at all. Uncovering my core wound and the beliefs and strategies it gave rise to, set me on the path of restoration and gave my life new meaning.

As much as we may think that our core beliefs and childhood experience have no real relevance in our adult lives, or want to just "get over it," it doesn't work that way. Because they are largely unconscious and live in the body itself as (cellular) memories, they can't be wished away or over-powered by the intellect.

I know from my experience of group work that virtually all of us share in a basic woundedness—we all get our ticket punched. Most of us have core beliefs and wounds that limit our ability to feel safe and okay just as we are. Many of us share a sense of insecurity and self-hatred.

I'm grateful for the opening and healing that self-awareness and self-acceptance have made possible in my life. It is this personal experience that inspires me to encourage others in the same direction.

Vulnerability

The key that unlocks the door to self-awareness and self-acceptance is an open and undefended state of consciousness that invites curiosity and self-reflection. We can call this way of being, this state of consciousness, *vulnerability*. When we are truly ready to meet the longing for deeper connection to ourselves, others, and life itself, the heart opens and the healing process begins in earnest.

Allowing ourselves to be vulnerable is an expression of our maturity and commitment to growth. Healing the relationship to self, we find that we no longer need to take everything so personally and defend ourselves from every perceived threat and insult. When, instead of responding in the habitual way, we practice staying with discomfort and fear as it arises, we change who we are in fundamental ways.

We don't grow by playing it safe and protecting the ego; we grow by exposing ourselves to consciousness itself and the transformative nature of life experience.

Defensiveness never worked anyway. We only end up creating and perpetuating what we try to defend against. For example, in trying to defend against our vulnerability, we will use a variety of strategies including denial, repression, aggression, projection, rationalization, and intellectualization. These, in turn, create more insecurity and fear, and the need for further defenses.

The heart must break open before we can become fully alive. We won't always like what we see and feel, but by embracing the "full catastrophe," as Zorba the Greek famously said, we free up life energy and step into our power and potential. Self-acceptance turns into acceptance of life on its own terms.

Separation is the unconscious default mode. Coming off automatic pilot we not only lay a foundation for a life that is more conscious, compassionate, and joyous, but we also see and experience our innate wholeness more clearly. It's an ongoing but nonlinear process. Expansion is often followed by contraction; one wall is torn down only to reveal the next. Coming back to our intention to grow and heal, we keep going, undaunted.

Shadow and Projection

> *Enlightenment is not found through imagining figures of light, but through making the darkness conscious.*
> — Carl Jung

Shadow and projection are two psychological mechanisms that demonstrate the consequences of not doing our inner work. We can think of the shadow as the unconscious aspects of the psyche—all the parts of ourselves of which we are not conscious. We operate day-to-day based not only on who we think we are—on aspects of ourselves of which we *are* conscious, but also based on other aspects of ourselves that remain completely hidden from our conscious awareness.

The shadow can include parts of us that we deem negative, bad, or otherwise socially unacceptable. These may be aspects of ourselves that are violent, cruel, crude, and racist, as well as the wild, untamed, and erotic aspects of ourselves that our culture so effectively represses.

Our deepest aspirations and most profound virtues can also be unconscious and be a part of our shadow. What we admire most in others is but a mirror reflecting our own potential—the greatness we fear and deny in ourselves. Insecurity, self-doubt, and shame can plunge qualities associated with a healthy sense of self into the shadow—qualities such as competence and a life-affirming sense of agency and autonomy.

We all have unconscious, disowned aspects of ourselves, and failing to consciously integrate them makes us more unpredictable and dangerous, not less. It's not uncommon to hear from a murderer's neighbor that he was "such a nice guy." And how destructive is it to have political leaders who so readily believe themselves to be "right" and "good," and yet remain unconscious of parts of themselves? Surely this lies at the core of much of the immaturity—the dishonesty, hypocrisy, and failure to take responsibility—we often see in politicians (and others).

On the other hand, disowning the energy of the "positive shadow" makes us less empowered and creative. It's easy to envy someone like Martin Luther King, Jr. and long for the next great leader to come along. But all those traits we most admire in Dr. King—eloquence, love, spiritual connection, and courage—are aspects of ourselves too!

How can we work with the shadow when it's unknown to us—when it's unconscious? We can start with the awareness that it's all just energy, and it's all already here, all the paradoxes of light and dark, spirit and body, sanity and insanity, the capacity to heal and to harm.

A next step can be to simply notice our annoyance with other people. The things that bother us in other people are often unowned or repressed parts of ourselves. Because what bothers us is seen as "not me," "bad," "wrong," or perhaps "too good" for us or otherwise unattainable, we get triggered into judgment and resentment. And here we're presented with a growth opportunity. The remedy for unconsciousness is consciousness. We can practice seeing and accepting that whatever it is that bothers us in other people—*everything* that bothers us—is a part of ourselves too. When we can see that and really take it in, the trigger disappears, the problem drops away, we can go about our own business and let other people go about theirs without self-righteousness or resentment.

This fits with my own experience. When I feel resentment toward someone wealthy, it has a lot to do with my own shadowy desire to have more than enough. When I get annoyed with a religious fundamentalist, it's my own inner fundamentalist given life as it's being *projected* onto the other person. By projecting certain qualities onto others, I can continue to deny them in myself.

Projection is one of the ways the shadow shows up on the surface of our lives. It is also one of the important reasons why we don't see others clearly for who they really are. Our beliefs shape and limit what we see—we see a version of others, colored by our own assumptions and beliefs.

Owning all our parts—with a humble bow to paradox, wholeness, and exquisite complexity—is the way to withdraw projections and bring awareness to our shadow. Rather than continue the cycle of unconsciousness, denial, and repression, we can embrace the unattractive parts as vital information—as energy directed at some longing or unmet need. For example, thoughts or acts of cruelty or violence often spring from a desperate longing for connection or safety. When the underlying need is brought into consciousness, attention is naturally directed inward and options for healthy responses become available. When the need stays unconscious, a victim mentality can prevail, with violence to ourselves and others the all too frequent result.

We can simplify things a great deal by just cutting to the chase and admitting that if it's out there—from tyrannical traits to saintly virtues—it's in us too. If everything is radically interconnected, how could it be otherwise? The question is: Is it conscious or unconscious? Is it on the way to being integrated as a part of our wholeness, or is it dangerously lurking in the shadows?

Although it can be uncomfortable, and the ego will resist the turn toward openness and honesty, life energy is freed and integrated when we do the work of owning all our parts. It's a step into vulnerability and the peace that comes with having nothing to hide, a step into fullness and maturity. And since this is deep work, you may want or need the support of wise and experienced elders or a professional therapist familiar with this type of work to help you navigate the psychic dark and return to the light with the gold.

Restorative Practice
Own Your Shadow

A poem by the Buddhist peacemaker Thich Nhat Hanh includes the following lines:

I am the frog swimming happily in the clear pond,
and I am also the grass-snake who, approaching in silence,
feeds itself on the frog.

I am the child in Uganda, all skin and bones,
my legs as thin as bamboo sticks,
and I am the arms merchant,
selling deadly weapons to Uganda.
I am the twelve-year-old girl, refugee on a small boat,

who throws herself into the ocean
after being raped by a sea pirate,
and I am the pirate, my heart not yet capable
of seeing and loving.

My joy is like spring, so warm
it makes flowers bloom in all walks of life.
My pain is like a river of tears, so full it fills the four oceans.

Please call me by my true names,
so I can hear all my cries and laughs at once,
so I can see that my joy and pain are one.

Please call me by my true names,
so I can wake up,
and so the door of my heart can be left open,
the door of compassion.[4]

The poem speaks to the reality of nonduality and those things we
tend to deny in ourselves and project onto others.

Take some time and reread the poem. Reflect on its mean-
ing and implications. Reflect on your own tendencies
toward separating characteristics out as good/bad, me/not
me. Reflect on your own tendencies toward self-righteousness.

Practice letting go of concepts of right/wrong, should/
shouldn't. Embrace reality just as it is. Relax your need to
control, to know, to be right, to be good. Just relax.

Open to and embrace your multi-faceted and paradoxical
nature. Take all your projections and bring them back into
yourself. Feel your own fullness and how you are a part of
the ebb and flow and wonderful mystery of life.

Open to the truth of interbeing, of not being separate from
anything, with no exceptions, no censorship. Notice if this
opens your heart.

"Meditation has been used for thousands of years across spiritual and religious traditions as a foundational mindfulness practice." "With meditation we develop a sense of being right here, right on the spot where we find ourselves. We become very simple, yet very dignified at the same time."

Chapter Five

Restoration's Foundation: Mindfulness

Humankind's survival depends on our ability to stop rushing.
—Thich Nhat Hahn

To move beyond the belief in separateness, it must be replaced with something else. Questioning the belief and opening to alternative realities can help soften the ground. Ultimately, however, only the lived experience of interrelatedness will suffice in replacing the belief in separateness.

Mindfulness is the practice that best facilitates the ability to feel the truth of interrelatedness. Mindfulness is the act of paying attention, in a conscious way, to the fullness of our experience— our *actual* experience as opposed to life on automatic pilot. It is a state of consciousness that comes with making a choice to be present to whatever is happening in the moment and holding that focus in a nonjudgmental way. It is, quite simply, the practice of *conscious* awareness.

Mindfulness is basic training for the brain, for the ability to put one's attention where one wants it, where it can do some good, not off, lost in a continual stream of repetitive thoughts. In each moment we have a choice as to where we place our attention, and this plays a big role in determining who we are and who we will become.

It has long been understood that the deepest truths about ourselves—our inherent wisdom and spiritual nature—are hidden from the rational mind. Mindfulness cultivates the knowing that transcends all the concepts and assumptions of the rational mind.

With mindfulness we bring a "witness " quality to our experience. We don't judge it or try to explain it. We just notice what we notice and let that be enough. What arises will shift and fade away and then something else will arise and we'll notice that. When we can stay in the present moment like this, we are in our power. The peacemaker lives right here in the present moment and looks with naked clarity at what is happening.

Mindfulness can be as simple as relaxing and noticing bodily sensations. It can be as simple as stopping while having breakfast, realizing you haven't been paying attention to what you're eating and drinking. And having stopped, beginning again with conscious awareness on the taste and look, the texture and aroma of the food and drink—the pleasing warmth of the mug in your hand. You can practice mindfulness anytime, anywhere. Talking, walking, eating, making love, standing in line—anytime is a good time to practice mindfulness.

While working a job that required a lot of driving, I discovered that the driving was boring only when I wasn't present to what was happening in the moment. If I wanted to be somewhere else, then it became a dull chore. If, instead, I was present to my body, to the feel of the car, the sounds, the temperature, and the landscape and the way it impacted me, then I felt alive and awake. The driving became yet another opportunity to be in the flow of life.

While mindfulness is simple and straightforward, it also takes practice. The untrained mind is relentless in its judging and commenting. And while this habitual activity of the mind is understandable and serves us to some degree, it can also be crazy-making and cut us off from our true nature, others, and the world.

Meditation: Cultivating Basic Sanity

Imagine being able to face any situation, including intense pain and even death, with openness and courage. Meditation cultivates these and other qualities by developing the nonresistance that allows our innate clarity and wisdom to shine forth.

Meditation has been used for thousands of years across spiritual and religious traditions as a foundational mindfulness practice. It includes many forms, but the core purpose, as with mindfulness in general, is to see and be with whatever is happening in an open and nonjudgmental way. The calmness and relaxation that often comes with meditation is a by-product of accepting our experience just as it is, which allows us to lower our defenses.

With meditation we develop a sense of being right here, right on the spot where we find ourselves. We become very simple, yet very dignified at the same time. The Tibetan meditation master Chögyam Trungpa called this cultivating *basic sanity*.

I was taught meditation by the Buddhist peacemaker Fleet Maull, who was a student of Chögyam Trungpa's and honed his meditation practice while serving a lengthy prison term. I went on to teach meditation at local jails as a volunteer for Fleet's organization, The Prison Mindfulness Institute. Some of the most satisfying experiences of my life came through sitting with groups of men in those noisy and chaotic environments and helping them connect with the inner peace that is always present underneath the thoughts.

It's funny how jails have figured so prominently in my experience of meditation. The first time I ever tried it I was sitting in a jail (without the "visitor" badge!). I had been arrested at a Greenpeace protest in New York City, and after about 30 hours of sitting around I had the idea to practice meditation. I didn't get very far along, however, before I was distracted by the sound of two guys arguing, one of whom turned out to be the only other Greenpeace person in the cell.

I went over to try to calm the situation down and before I knew it I was getting punched in the mouth and sliced at with a small razor blade. That led to some drastic maneuvers to get us both out of there as fast as possible and brought an abrupt conclusion to my first meditation session.

I remember the day, many years later, when I decided to take charge of where I put my attention while meditating. This had been encouraged in meditation class many times but I had never really taken the leap; I was still very caught up in identification with my thoughts. On this particular day, however, I set a clear intention to not get caught by the thoughts and I followed through with that, and those moments of feeling in control of my mind were a revelation.

In my late-forties I was finally taking charge of my mind and my life! It was a direct taste of the freedom that comes with taking responsibility for where I put my attention and what I do with my thoughts.

Continued practice has helped calm my mind enough that I have begun to be able to be aware of awareness itself. I've experienced awareness as my most basic capacity as a human being. It is there to experience in any moment, and when I do, it puts any thought, belief, feeling, or emotion into the larger context of my true nature. As this awareness, I am close to the Ground of Being and know myself to be already—perfectly—whole and sane.

Restorative Practice
Sitting Meditation

While there are many different ways to meditate, the most basic practice is to follow the breath. Holding your breath is the quickest way to demonstrate the importance of the breath. And yet, because it happens without conscious effort, we tend to pay it little attention.

The breath forms a natural bridge between body and mind. This makes it a compelling focus for meditation. In continually making the choice to come back to the breath, we exercise our awareness muscles. We learn that we have choice over where we place our attention. As we practice witnessing our thoughts and not getting caught by them, we discover that we are not our thoughts. Through meditation we connect with the silence that is already present underneath all the noise created by our thoughts.

Make a commitment to sit for a certain length of time—twenty to thirty minutes is a good amount of time for beginning meditators. It can help to set an alarm so you don't have to worry about when the time is up. Take a comfortable sitting posture. You don't need a special cushion—a chair works fine as long as your feet are on the ground or floor.

Bring awareness to your posture. A straight back will help you breathe more easily and bring dignity to your practice. "Strong back and soft front" is a helpful reminder.

Relax your mouth and face—this will help relax the whole body. You can have your eyes open or closed. If open, place a soft focus on the floor about four to eight feet in front of you.

Sit in such a way that you are comfortable and present. From a place of relaxation and alertness, allow your awareness to settle from your head down through your neck and shoulders, through your chest and into your belly. Let your awareness settle like sand thrown into a pond.

Feel the support of the Earth and let yourself become simple and open. Take your time. Then begin to follow your breath.

Put your full awareness on following your breath, the in breath and the out breath. Place your attention on the breath moving down in the belly. Don't change your breath—just follow it as it naturally is.

When a thought arises, simply notice it and say silently and gently to yourself, "thinking," and bring your awareness back to the breath. Don't give the thought any extra energy by trying to understand or judge it. Evaluations of yourself and how well you're doing at meditation are just more thoughts, so here again, just name it as "thinking" and return to the breath.

> *Continue this process of making the choice to come back to the breath. Remain a simple witness to the flow of thoughts that come and go. There is nothing to do, no goal. You're not trying to change anything. Just keep coming back to the breath.*
>
> *Effort only gives the mind more to do. Rest in the peace and openness that is naturally there.*
>
> *When the allotted time is up, take a few moments to notice the pure awareness that is present. Take it in. Then, make a conscious, mindful transition into your next activity.*

The Fearful Brain

A basic understanding of the brain's structure and function underscores the value of mindfulness practice. The brain consists of three main parts: the brain stem, the limbic system, and the neocortex. The brain stem is central to the control of many basic bodily functions such as circulation and respiration. In terms of evolution, this is the oldest part of the brain and is sometimes referred to as the reptilian brain.

The limbic system (the paleomammalian brain) developed as reptiles evolved into mammals. Among other things, the limbic system is involved in memory, the impulse to connect with others, the fight-flight-freeze response, and other emotional responses. The neocortex (the neomammalian brain) plays a key role in the "higher" rational functions such as language, planning, and abstract thought. It is associated with the evolution of primates, and comprises about 80% of the human brain. The neocortex gives us the ability to be thoughtful, respectful, and kind.

The pre-rational limbic system is the fast circuit and the default "decider" whenever we believe we are threatened. But while the limbic system operates much faster and more automatically than the neocortex, it can "listen" to the neocortex. Because it is emotion-based, the non-rational limbic system listens best under conditions of safety. This is why we function most thoughtfully and maturely when we are feeling calm and safe.

The rub is that the brain is naturally oriented toward survival, not calmness. Paul Shepard put this in evolutionary perspective: "As surely as we hear the blood in our ears, the echoes of a million midnight shrieks of monkeys, whose last sight of the world was the eyes of a panther, have their traces in our nervous systems."[1]

We know the truth of the fearful brain from our own experience. We know how fast we react to unfamiliar and possibly threatening sounds, sensations, and situations. We know that we can be so preoccupied with threat that we often don't fully enjoy even our most pleasurable experiences. Instead of savoring something nourishing, we move out of the present moment and start thinking about how it won't last or could be better, the next bad thing that could happen, or the next thing we have to do.

The fearful brain also shows up in the way we tend to make painful experiences worse with the many layers of thinking and stories we pile on. With physical pain, we tend to tighten our whole body in aversion and thereby amplify our suffering. The pain associated with the breakup of a relationship is worsened many times over by the endless storylines about who's to blame and all our regrets, resentments, and rationalizations. Mindfulness helps to soothe the emotional mind, calming the limbic system's orientation toward threat and defense.

There is a very physical explanation for how mindfulness practice benefits the brain. It is still relatively recently that the brain has been shown to generate new neural connections throughout life, based on experience and learning. This finding, known as *neuroplasticity*, explains how it's possible to break even the oldest habits and patterns. The basic mechanism is this: where attention goes, neurons fire; and where neurons fire together, they wire together. It's this wiring together that creates new neural pathways that change the structure of the brain.

If attention is placed on doing something different, like not following the automatic impulse to respond in anger when anger arises, a new neural pathway option is created. If, through conscious intention and choice, the mind is drawn back repeatedly to this new response, the new pathway is strengthened and can eventually start to compete with the old pathway—the old way of thinking and behaving. More choice in how we respond is created. We change the brain and therefore ourselves in a very real and practical way.

The Benefits of Mindfulness

Between stimulus and response there is a space.
In that space is our power to choose our response.
In our response lies our growth and our future.
— Victor Frankl

With mindfulness we work the gap between stimulus and response. We acknowledge what's present—feelings, thoughts, emotions, sensations, memories—without attaching to it, without the need for an immediate response. This allows us to distinguish between what's really happening—the raw data—and our projections and stories about what's happening. We get an additional choice beyond "stewing or spewing," and that choice begins with simply noticing what's really happening.

Mindfulness cultivates many qualities essential for restoration, including openness, discernment, concentration, and an overall sense of wellbeing. Mindfulness, especially through meditation practices, has been shown to improve memory, learning, and physical health—benefiting the immune system, blood pressure, asthma symptoms, and chronic pain.[2] Mindfulness helps prevent relapse of depression and drug addiction, and is effective at reducing symptoms of anxiety, post-traumatic stress disorder, and obsessive-compulsive disorder.[3]

As the foundation for emotional intelligence, the self-awareness that mindfulness cultivates allows the neocortex to mediate the limbic system's fight-flight-freeze response.

Mindfulness is thus a vehicle for the natural, organic unfolding toward greater maturity and wisdom that is every person's birthright.

Mindfulness cultivates three other qualities worthy of special mention: courage, freedom, and resilience. Mindfulness builds the capacity to be present to fear without needing to distract or numb ourselves. The ability to stay with fear, to stay with discomfort and insecurity, gives rise to freedom—freedom from the limitations of our preconceived ideas and concepts. These capacities, in turn, lead to the ability to face any situation with more resilience.

Even our ideas about death are only ideas. Once we begin to see beyond ideas and concepts to the true nature of reality—that all life arises from and then returns to the Ground of Being, and that the spiritual essence, the essential spark of life, remains unchanged in the process—we come to understand that there really is no beginning and no end. *This* is the greatest source of courage, freedom, and resilience.

We could add happiness to the list of benefits as well. In the present moment, without attachments, cravings, and aversions, everything is perfect just as it is and we naturally feel more happiness and joy. As long as we are alive and paying attention, there is beauty to appreciate and wonder to behold. And when we are not feeling so good we can deal with that too—when we pay attention—with less fear and suffering.

Restorative Practice
Mindful Walking

At meditation retreats, periods of sitting are often interspersed with walking meditation. In walking meditation, the meditator lifts one foot at a time, very slowly, with full awareness on the feet. It is a practice that synchronizes mind and body, and places us, firmly but lightly, on the Earth.

Mindful walking is a more general practice that can be used anytime we are walking. Any activity can be done with mindfulness and, in my experience, walking is one of the most satisfying.

Begin by simply noticing how it feels in your body to walk. Notice any aches or pains, the aliveness and energy. Notice your surroundings. Take it all in.

When you are ready, move your attention into your feet. Feel your feet on the Earth, notice the way the Earth supports you with every step. Notice how it feels to walk in a conscious, reverent way.

While keeping your attention lightly on the inner sense of walking, gradually expand your awareness to include your environment. For example, feel the air on your skin and notice the temperature. Then turn your attention toward the quality of the light or the sounds around you. All the while staying present to the walking itself.

Place your attention on things in a conscious way. You can imagine that you are walking as carefully and patiently as a mountain lion stalking deer in a forest. Enjoy your animal body. When something draws your attention, a bird for example, stop walking so you can be with the bird fully. When you are ready, continue walking.

Practice staying present to the walking at all times, the feel of it in your body. As you wind down the practice, notice the energy and aliveness pulsing through you.

Rediscovering the Wisdom of Our Bodies

Throughout this book I have tried to resist the temptation to make declarations about what we "have to," "must," or "should" do. I don't think life works that way. But in the context of restoration, I have made what I think are some defensible exceptions. Reconnecting with the body and our *felt sense* is one of them. I know this has been absolutely essential on my healing journey. When the marriage counselor asked me what I was feeling and I didn't know, I began to understand just how cut off I was from myself, and how that disconnection was related to others.

When we give enough sustained attention to the body to really notice what we feel, we connect with the felt sense. It might be a feeling of warmth, agitation, constriction, ease, or a thousand other sensations. If mindfulness is the act of noticing, the felt sense is that which is noticed. Combined, they allow us to engage with the world in a conscious and reciprocal way.

As part of the life-denying worldview, the mind has long been elevated and considered separate from the body. This has led to deeply engrained patterns of disembodiment. The mind-body split helps to uphold other splits, such as the belief that humans are separate from each other and the Earth. A lack of depth in our experiencing is what allows the belief in separateness to carry forward from generation to generation.

When we pay attention to the felt sense, we go deeper than the thoughts and concepts which are always secondary to actual experience. With the felt sense, we go on direct, unadulterated experience. We get at the real truth of what is happening in the moment. It's a different kind of knowing, a knowing with our whole being. The body is the ultimate source of our most radical truth telling.

As we learn to inhabit our bodies more consciously, we can continue to take the mountain lion as our guide. She is fully present in the moment and her body. She can't afford to daydream about tomorrow or feel entitled to her next meal—she knows with her whole being that it must be earned. Her full embodiment is the key to survival for her and her cubs.

Our survival too, now seems to require this level of attunement with our bodies. Mindfulness and the felt sense allow us to distinguish between feelings and emotions, between what we can actually feel in the body and the thoughts that take us over in response to direct experience. A focus on what can be felt in the body keeps us connected to what is really happening, as opposed to what we "think" is happening. Feelings keep us in the present moment, emotions keep us in the past or future.

Emotions tend to be linked to early experience. This is why the response is so often exaggerated, so disproportionate to the stimulus. Emotions are often based on the perceived need to protect or defend ourselves and limit our perspective and our ability to stay open. They put us in a story of right and wrong, good and bad, pleasant and unpleasant. In contrast, feelings ground us in the present moment where there is no story, and help us stay open and vulnerable. We can still protect ourselves if that's what is needed, but we can do it from a place of integrity and choice.

By helping us to reconnect with the wisdom of our bodies, by bringing us more alive and awake, mindfulness is a re-wilding of the self. When we get in touch with the life energy that moves in us and longs for expression, reintegration of our whole being takes place. This unleashes the imagination and all kinds of potential. Here we enter the realm of relationships, stories, dreams, and poetry with no censorship. The writer Terry Tempest Williams concludes her beautiful book, *Desert Quartet: An Erotic Landscape,* with these lines:

There is no need to speak.

Listen.

Below us.

Above us.

Inside us.

Come.

This is all there is.

Restorative Practice
Feel the Felt Sense

Connecting with your felt sense simply means becoming very present to your body and noticing the feelings and sensations that are there. When you get curious about what is happening in your body, you may find that the ability to really feel the subtleties is not well developed. Like so many others, you may have taken the body for granted and not listened to it for so long that it can take some practice to feel deeply into the body once again. That's okay, that's why it's called practice. Start right where you are without shame or judgment.

The following exercise is easiest to practice when you are feeling upset or experiencing noticeable physical pain—simply because there can seem to be more sensation to notice.

Let your mind get quiet and place your attention fully in the body. Direct your attention inward and notice what you notice. Be curious and welcoming toward whatever arises. If you don't notice anything, just continue to stay present to the body. If many feelings arise, notice that and then watch where your attention goes from there.

Get underneath all thinking and emotion by bringing curiosity to the sensations themselves. Questions directed to the body, the felt sense itself, and not the head can help:

What, exactly, is the sensation? Where do I notice it? What are its qualities?

If there is numbness, what does the numbness feel like?

Is there pain or discomfort? Is it familiar?

What is this feeling telling me? Is there a met or unmet need giving rise to this feeling?

When the mind wanders off just bring your attention back to the feeling. Let your awareness be with the body in an open and intuitive way; don't get trapped in trying to figure anything out. Let a different kind of knowing arise.

Stay with the practice long enough to make it a workout for your awareness, but don't overdo it.

Before transitioning out of the exercise, notice the overall quality of your awareness and the energy present. How does it feel to even try to connect with the wisdom of the body?

Set an intention to continue this practice periodically throughout the day. Notice if you feel yourself coming more fully alive.

Basic Goodness

A big part of the restoration that comes with mindfulness practice is the result of connecting with our own basic goodness. In a culture where shame and self-hate are epidemic, the realization that we, all of us, possess an innate basic goodness is a key that frees us from many toxic beliefs. Chögyam Trungpa wrote:

> Unless we can discover that ground of goodness in our own lives, we cannot hope to improve the lives of others....When we feel that our lives are genuine and good, we do not have to deceive ourselves or other people. We can see our own shortcomings without feeling guilty or inadequate.[4]

An appreciation for basic goodness is exemplified in Sister Helen Prejean's work with death row inmates, as depicted in the film *Dead Man Walking*. She understands that every person is worth more than their worst mistake. I remember how I sat up and took note when Fleet Maull, reflecting on his years in prison, spoke about finding basic goodness in even the hardest of men.

My own experience working in jails and institutions has convinced me of the truth of basic goodness. I've worked with some seriously wounded people who have done very harmful things, and I have always been able to connect with them, human being to human being. Our shared longings and humanity are the great equalizers.

Everyone wants to feel safe and be happy, to relax and feel at ease. Toxic thoughts and harmful behaviors are overlays that are always there for a reason. A practice such as animal-assisted therapy, which is often used in jails and prisons, is as effective as it is because even the most traumatized people long for love and connection.

This topic reminds me of the stories I've heard from people who were with someone at the moment of their death. My uncle Greg told me a story a long time ago about being the first one on the scene of a very bad car accident. After calling for an ambulance he crawled into one of the cars where a young woman lay dying. It was clear to Greg that she was hanging on to life by the thinnest of threads. He followed his instinct to just hold her and speak to her softly. The moment she died, he felt something leave her body.

Greg told me that the shift was dramatic. One moment, he was holding a living, animated human being, and in the next, a dead body. Whatever that was that left her body at the moment of death, it made all the difference. While I don't necessarily equate basic goodness with that most essential spark of life, I do imagine it to be just as fundamental to our humanness.

Basic goodness doesn't create a utopia where everyone is harmless and honest. It does not justify hurtful behavior. What an appreciation of basic goodness *does* do is encourage us to look at ourselves and others differently, even those who have caused tremendous harm. If we are not going to write other people off, we will naturally be more curious about who they are and what led them to cause harm in the first place. And if we do the work of owning our own shadows, we will know that we too are capable, under the right circumstances, of causing serious harm.

The Transpersonal Dimensions of Mindfulness

Human development and maturation can be said to move through three primary stages: pre-personal, personal, and transpersonal. In the pre-personal stage, we are born unsocialized and without a sense of independent self. Later, with the personal stage, we are enculturated and learn the norms and values of society. This includes developing our individuality and the functional aspects of ego. It also includes absorbing the belief in separateness that comes with the dominant worldview.

Human development often ends here, with conventional belief and value systems going unchallenged. But as the Perennial Philosophy and the three-stage model of development suggest, the transpersonal stage lies beyond the personal as an open field for realizing true maturity and our spiritual essence as human beings.

In the Buddhist tradition, the belief that we are separate entities with solidity, independence, and permanence, is seen as the ultimate source of our suffering. Leading with the ego, the sense of "me," we seek comfort and security at all costs. Coming from a place of fear, we employ the full force of our intellects to avoid change and uncertainty. But since we are embedded in a reality characterized by groundlessness and impermanence, all attempts at finding solidity and security are destined to fail.

Without mindfulness, revelations of our true nature can manifest in a thousand ways every day and we simply won't notice them. Mindfulness helps us find the stability to grapple with life's bigger questions: Who am I? How is this miracle of life made possible? Have I lived fully? What happens when we die?

The path of restoration is ultimately a mystical journey, an ever-deepening embrace of the groundless nature of reality and the truth of interbeing. We discover that the world does not consist of "things" with any real permanence, but is instead characterized by a moment–to–moment unfolding of energies and forms in constant motion. With this understanding, the mind settles and we find more gratitude for things just as they are. We can relax and release our stranglehold on all sorts of attachments—to preferred outcomes and other preferences, to desires, cravings, aversions, habits, and fears. This is true freedom.

Restorative Practice
Cultivate a Larger Sense of Self

The real crux of our restoration and healing lies in dissolving the belief in separateness through the lived experience of pure awareness. Pure awareness is our true nature; it is the essential gift of being human.

Pure awareness is the source of the love and compassion that flow so freely when the heart is open. Awareness is what allows us to experience interbeing as a lived reality.

Transformation comes when we keep pulling the rug out from under the ego. We open to who we are beyond fear and insecurity, beyond thought and thinking. Then we open some more. Standing in the truth of how the world actually works, with insight into the essence of ourselves and all things, we find the inspiration we need to fuel the transformational journey.

All mindfulness practices serve to cultivate a larger sense of self. In this exercise we go directly to the heart of it with a very straightforward inquiry. As with all the practices in this book, move through the steps at a pace that works for you.

Choose a time for this practice when you will be able to focus without distraction, ideally for at least 30 minutes. Take a comfortable sitting posture. Connect with the breath.

Notice the way the breath comes naturally, without any effort—without any "doing" on your part, life is breathing you. Life is living you. You are but a witness.

Stay with this witness quality. When thoughts and distractions arise, gently come back to the breath, back to being pure awareness.

Ask yourself, "What else is there in this moment except for pure awareness?"

"Is this the truth of who I am underneath the surface of thought?"

"Is this 'what' I am beyond all superficial labels and identities?

"Is it true that right now in this moment, without interference from thoughts, that everything is perfect just as it is?"

Stay with the breath. Stay with the awareness. There are no "right" answers. There aren't really even any questions— only awareness.

When you start to feel complete, notice the quality of your being in this moment. If there is an expanded sense of self, take that in. If there isn't, don't make that into a problem.

Whatever your experience, consider repeating this practice on a regular basis. Make it more and more spacious, giving yourself time to take in the information and knowing that comes.

Move into your next activity in a conscious way.

"*When we see ourselves as part of a greater whole we become stronger and more resilient. Many of us have experienced the way that being out in nature puts our lives into perspective.*" "*With the shift toward participation and reciprocity we need never feel alone.*"

Chapter Six

Restoring Our Relationship to Nature

You didn't come into this world. You came out of it,
like a wave from the ocean. You are not a stranger here.
— Alan Watts

Along with our essence as spiritual beings with great potential to expand our sense of self beyond the limits of ego, our non-separation from nature stands out as a basic truth of our existence.

The feelings of peacefulness and ease that wash over us as we relax in an open field, a forest, or on a beach don't come from the sense of being alone and separate. They come through intimate communion with the sights and sounds, the smells, and the presence of trees, birds, waves, sand, sky, and breeze.

In moments of quiet contemplation outdoors, we are just doing what we were designed to do. Body, senses, mind, and soul are exercised and our wholeness is expressed without effort because we are of the Earth and we belong here.

Pondering our evolutionary context can be helpful in understanding our rootedness in the Earth. The Old Stone Age (the Paleolithic period) began approximately three million years ago and ended 12,000 years ago. It thus accounts for more than 99.5% of human and proto-human existence.[1] Using an estimate that modern humans have existed in more or less their present form for 200,000 years (and using 30 years to represent a generation), we find that 6,667 generations have come before us and passed on their genetic makeup, unconscious habits, and learned cultural ways. The number of generations since the shift to agriculture took place is 333; and it has only been eleven generations since Isaac Newton established the basis for the mechanistic worldview.

An evolutionary perspective makes it clear that however deep the roots of the life-denying worldview may be, our roots in the Earth are deeper still. The connection to the natural world is still a fundamental aspect of who we are, regardless of how dormant and unconscious it has become. Making that connection as conscious as possible is now one of our most important tasks.

Restorative Practice
Write Your Eco-Biography[2]

Writing your eco-biography can be a good way to deepen your appreciation for your interbeing with nature and the way the natural world has helped shape who you are. Do it with mindfulness as a contemplative practice.

Find a quiet place outdoors to reflect on your life and take some notes. Stay connected to your breath and body and feel the way the Earth is supporting you right now. Let the natural world fill and hold you.

Notice your experience as it arises—there may be sadness or anger, joy or longing. Stay connected to your heart—this is not an intellectual exercise. When you feel ready, ask yourself:

"What are my earliest memories of nature?"

"What landscapes and weather do I most remember?" "What are some specific experiences I remember?"

"What trees, plants, birds, and animals do I remember most deeply?" "What memories come to mind?"

"How did my early experiences with the natural world shape me as a child and who I am today?"

"What is my relationship to nature now?" "Do I have a special place in nature that touches me deeply?"

"What feelings have come up as I do this exercise?" "What do these feelings tell me?"

Take the information that comes through this process and spend some time writing it down as your eco-biography. This is the story of how the Earth has impacted and shaped you. It is the story of your relationship to your truest home and the other beings you share it with.

Consequences of the Human/Nature Split

The negative consequences of the human/nature split—the belief that we as human beings are separate from nature—can hardly be overstated. This split has stifled our full humanness and ability to feel at home in the Earth. The result is a psychic homelessness that undermines our health, happiness, and chances for long-term survival.

Not only has the human/nature split damaged our ability to know who we are, without a deep connection to place—to the local environment and the Earth as a whole—we can't really know where we are. This separateness causes and perpetuates psychological dis-ease in the form of numbness, dissatisfaction, insecurity, fear, and an emptiness that cannot be filled by material goods and distractions.

The more we try to fill this wounded, empty place inside us with stuff, the worse we feel. The focus on materialism just pulls us further from what we are really longing for—a sense of wholeness, an intimacy with life itself.

Much of the psychopathology in evidence today can be attributed to the human/nature split. The symptoms include drug abuse, obesity, excessive materialism, powerlessness, attention deficit disorder, hyperactivity, depression, narcissism, and immaturity.[3] Without an engaged and intimate relationship with the natural world, healthy human development is thwarted and we get sick. However well kept the secret, our sanity is inextricably tied to the Earth.

As already mentioned, the original meaning of the word *insane* is "not whole." In the language of the Okanagan, an indigenous tribe of North America, the word insanity includes four syllables.

The first syllable describes the tendency to "talk, talk inside your head," the second to "being scattered and having no community," the third to "having no relationship to the land," and the fourth to "being disconnected from the whole-earth part" of ourselves.[4] I think many of us can relate to these expressions of disconnection.

Without a conscious, participatory, and reciprocal relationship with the Earth, there can be no wholeness, no true sanity. According to Jeanette Armstrong, who is Okanagan:

> Okanagans teach that the body is the Earth itself. They say that our flesh, blood, and bones are Earth-body; in all cycles in which the Earth moves, so does our body. We are everything that surrounds us, including the vast forces we only glimpse. If we cannot maintain and stay in balance with the outer self, then we cannot continue as an individual life-form, and we dissipate back into the larger self.[5]

In other words, if we don't get back into balance with the Earth, our insanity will lead us to extinction!

Nature has always been humanity's primary teacher. Nature provides the basic context for our lives and the laws that guide us most truly in how to live. Sitting at the base of an old tree or mountain, we sit at the feet of elders. Watching and listening to a flock of wild geese high overhead we get inspiration and lessons in strength, determination, cooperation, and much more.

I once witnessed a group of a dozen large mule deer bucks in the woods as they walked by me single file. They seemed determined to not let me interfere with their daily routine.

They were so impressive, so sleek and muscular and potent in their "buckness." I sat there completely humbled and inspired by the way they held themselves. I related to their strength, dignity, and other qualities as a felt sense. My own buckness came alive and lifted me up. The whole world became more sane and meaningful as I watched them go by.

We are a species designed to appreciate and celebrate the Earth in all its diversity as the dance of form and formlessness unfolds before us. Unfortunately, our ability to play this role as a conscious participant, witness, and storyteller has been damaged by the belief in separateness.

Losing the sense of interbeing with all that exists also hinders the discovery of our spiritual essence as human beings. Stuck in insecurity, fear, and a scarcity mentality—not knowing who or where we really are—the small, ego-based self gets all the attention. We don't grow up and we don't grow down.

Because it is an aspect of the life-denying worldview, the human/nature split doesn't discriminate. There are few among us who have fully healed themselves of it. We can watch out for the tendency to use this split as another excuse to judge others and feel superior: "I'm working to get over my belief in separateness but they are still clueless."

Mindfulness and Nature-Based Practice

Even though I was fortunate to have had early, formative experiences with oceans, mountains, and deserts, I still know the depth of the human/nature split on a very personal level. Despite the early connections and being fed by time in the natural world my entire adult life, I've come to realize the limits of my relationship to nature. I realize it, for example, in reflecting on the many backpacking trips into the wilderness where I relished the quiet and the sense of being alone. Alone, despite the hundreds of trees and birds, the countless number of plants and insects, and the living rivers. I knew these things were present and I enjoyed them, but I didn't have a mindful relationship with them. I wasn't participating with the natural world in a conscious way, and nature dissolved into a kind of backdrop for my own personal dramas.

It stills happens. Most days I go for a walk in my neighborhood. Some days I walk but stay almost completely in my head, like I'm floating around in a bubble. Other days I pay much more attention to what is around me. These more mindful walks become a communion with my non-human neighbors and a celebration of the world's beauty. When I'm paying attention, there is usually something that will bring me to my knees in awe and reverence—the whimsical textures of sycamore bark, the nimble notes of warbler song, the ominous beauty of a high-stacked cumulonimbus cloud. The simple act of a 45-minute walk results in a noticeable shift—fresh energy pours in and I feel more grounded, grateful, and connected. Mindfulness makes all the difference.

Nature is the perfect place to practice moment-to-moment awareness. When we slow down and sit still, we can best experience the more elusive sights and sounds of nature, the weasel stealthily working a fallen tree on the hunt for chipmunks, the coyote perfectly blended with the tall grass ready to pounce on a vole, the sound of worms moving under the leaves, the melodies of birds in the distance.

The unpredictability of nature encourages us to see with fresh eyes. We can practice different ways of knowing by letting go of our labels and preconceived ideas. When we can see each thing in its own right—blackbird, ponderosa pine, boulder—we see it more clearly as an ever changing presence with a uniqueness all its own.

Coming into the present moment brings aliveness to our senses. In the now we are simply what we are and always have been, conscious animals living on the luscious Earth. Reconnecting with the Earth becomes a natural process and not something we have to force.

Restorative Practice
Nature as Mirror

Because of our interbeing, we can see and feel ourselves reflected in everything in nature—the eagle, hawk, and songbird, the smallest insect and tallest mountain. If we pay close enough attention to an oak tree, we can see ourselves reflected in the oak's rootedness and strong trunk, the reach for the sky, the ability to survive storms and drought. Like us, the tree is marked by life but keeps on growing.

We can offer our questions and our pain to nature, listen for guidance and find unwavering support.

For this exercise, plan to spend at least three hours of contemplative time in nature. Choose a natural setting with a river, creek, or an impressive tree. While everything in nature can mirror our experience, I have found rivers and trees to be exceptional for this exercise. Choose a place where you will have some solitude and also feel safe and relaxed.

Mark the beginning of this time in nature with a simple ceremony, some gesture that says, "Now it begins." It could be as basic as finding a fallen tree or branch to step over and, in crossing that threshold you enter a different way of knowing and hold to the truth of your interbeing with all that you see.

Find a place to stay still and enter into relationship with, in this example, a river.

Once you settle in, use all your senses to experience the different aspects of the river. Let the river show you its personalities and essence.

Take your time and practice seeing the river with fresh eyes.

When you feel ready, shift your focus and let the river be a mirror of your life, your personalities and essence. Don't make it an intellectual exercise, just open to the organic exchange between your being and the river.

Can you see yourself reflected in the meandering quality of the river, in rapids and falls, in the bright light reflecting off the surface, and in the dark, shadowy places?

Do you see aspects of yourself in the river's ability to meet resistance with persistence and ease, and in the determination to keep going, to merge with the sea, the source?

Does the spilling over of banks at flood and the stagnation during low water speak to your own extremes?

Can you see the water and blood of your own body reflected in the river?

Keep coming back to the river as mirror. Stay patient and open. Stay with "being" and let go of "doing."

As the time you have dedicated to this practice winds down, notice what the experience has left you with. Notice any thoughts, feelings, sensations, or images that stand out. If nothing happened, don't worry about it. Understand that a practice like this may be exercising new muscles of awareness and try it again some other time.

End with a simple ceremonial act that says, "Now it ends." (For example, stepping back over the fallen tree or branch you may have stepped over to begin the exercise.)

Participation and Reciprocity

Whether we are conscious of it or not, in every moment and with every breath we participate directly in the world. We watch and are watched, touch and are touched. Our existence from the very beginning is dependent on our participation with the Earth. Whether we live in New York City or a ranch in Montana, there is never a nanosecond of separation.

Indigenous cultures continue to be informed by the felt sense of participation and reciprocity. In the indigenous worldview, all beings, the land itself, and the cosmos as a whole participate in the flow of life in a dynamic way. When the famous researcher Jane Goodall asked a group of Mestizo Indians from the Peruvian rainforest how they distinguished plants that are healing from those that are potentially dangerous, they were perplexed. To them the answer was so obvious: they listen to the plants.[6]

For our earliest ancestors and the indigenous people of today, the land is not a landscape to be admired from a psychic distance but a true home to be inhabited intimately. Plants, animals, and the land engage with the human mind and senses in open dialogue. Such a participatory and reciprocal relationship with nature is everyone's heritage and birthright—we all have indigenous roots.

Reciprocity is an ancient principle and practice that reflects interconnectedness and the cyclical nature of things. Christianity's Golden Rule, with its injunction to "Do unto others as you would have them do unto you," expresses reciprocity and is found in some form in almost every religion and ethical tradition.[7] It is the give and take of reciprocity that allows life to flourish over time.

Never in the course of evolution has it been so critical for humans to find ways to live on the Earth that are reciprocal, or to use Thomas Berry's phrase, "mutually-enhancing." The idea of mutual enhancement highlights how far we have to go. It emphasizes that the challenge goes beyond minimizing impacts to actually enhancing the life-giving capacity of the Earth. This means that virtually everything we do on a large scale—transportation, agriculture, energy production, to name just a few examples—must be done very differently.

Reciprocity toward the Earth can include such things as improving soil fertility and water and air quality, replanting forests, and protecting habitat—all in an ongoing way. Removing dams on salmon rivers such as Oregon's Elwha (which was done!) is another great example. We receive; we give back.

The biologist John Todd's system of wastewater treatment is often cited as an innovative and elegant example of mutual enhancement. Todd developed a living aquatic system of fish, plants, snails, and other organisms that feed on and clean human sewage to such an extent that the water coming out of the system is drinkable. The nutrients in the sewage support the plants, fish, and other animals. The fish, as well as the flowers, lettuce, and tomatoes grown can be used by humans. The system mimics a natural wetland and is self-perpetuating. Todd used a similar concept, based on nature's own design, to successfully treat highly toxic wastes from a Superfund site in Chattanooga, Tennessee.[8]

Mutual enhancement stands in stark contrast to attempts to minimize and mitigate environmental harm. The end result of the minimize/mitigate approach is invariably degradation of one degree or another that creeps forward from project to project, year to year, with the periodic eco-catastrophe thrown in for good measure. There is no enhancement.

The pioneering conservationist Aldo Leopold wrote, "Examine each question in terms of what is ethically and esthetically right, as well as what is ecologically expedient. A thing is right when it tends to preserve the integrity, stability, and beauty of the biotic community. It is wrong when it tends otherwise."[9] Leopold's words remain a good guide in reestablishing a reciprocal relationship with the Earth.

Every act of conscious participation and reciprocity with nature helps to retrain us back into healthy relationship with life. It is not too late to demonstrate that we have the intelligence and creativity required to continue our evolutionary journey here on Earth.

Restorative Practice
Reciprocity

This exercise focuses on experiencing reciprocity directly. Plan to spend at least three hours in a natural setting you feel comfortable in.

As you begin the exercise, start by using all your senses to experience your surroundings and the other beings present in a full and deep way. Hear the sounds and allow them to penetrate your every cell. Use your sense of smell to sense who and what is there. Find something to touch and taste. Be the observer taking it all in with the body.

Then shift into being the one who is observed. If the very essence of form is energy, if every atom and cell has intelligence, then every "thing" you see and hear and sense, has its own life force energy and consciousness. Everything you experience has a way of experiencing you.

Let yourself be seen and heard and felt. Instead of you touching the tree, the tree now touches you. Instead of you sitting on the Earth as the actor, now the Earth is the actor as she supports you.

How does it feel to be seen and felt and experienced by nature in this way? Is there a felt sense of it in your body? Can you feel the two-way exchange of energy?

Move back and forth between being a human experiencing nature and being a human experienced by nature. Touch and be touched. Hear and be heard. See and be seen. Feel how you are not alone. Continue to come back to the senses as a way to stay present and connected.

Notice if there is a felt sense of interrelatedness present. Go into your body and soften your grip on the belief in separateness. Where do you make the cut between self and other? Where does the tree end and begin? Where do you end and begin?

As you transition out of this practice, take some slow, deep breaths. Notice the spacious quality of your mind. Notice how it feels to be a part of nature in this moment.

Evidence for the Healing Benefits of Nature

With the shift toward participation and reciprocity we need never feel alone. When we see ourselves as part of a greater whole we become stronger and more resilient. Many of us have experienced the way that being out in nature puts our lives into perspective. Whether it's the vastness of an ocean, the grandeur of high mountain peaks, the silvery thread of a creek, or the singing of birds—the spell our problems can cast over us is easily broken by direct contact with the natural world.

A growing body of scientific evidence is confirming what common sense already knows—contact with nature is physically, psychologically, and spiritually healthy for us. Some of the proven benefits include:

- Reductions in stress, anxiety, fatigue, obesity, anger, and depression;

- Increases in optimism, self-esteem, vitality, memory, attention span, creativity, and overall work productivity;

- In children, reductions in the symptoms of attention-deficit disorder; and

- In hospital settings, patients with a view of the natural world have shown decreases in preoperative anxiety and postoperative recovery time, as well as decreases in painkiller use and overall complaints.[10]

Even in the unlikely environment of a Nazi prison camp, nature has worked its healing magic. The psychiatrist Victor Frankl tells a story about a conversation he had with a young female prisoner who was cheerful despite her expectation of imminent death.

This woman told Frankl she was grateful "fate has hit me so hard. In my former life I was spoiled and did not take spiritual accomplishments seriously." She went on to say that the lone chestnut tree outside the window of her hut, of which she could see but a single branch, was her only friend and that she often spoke to it. Frankl asked if the tree replied. She said yes, the tree said to her "I am here—I am here—I am life, eternal life."[11]

My own healing journey with nature has taken many twisting turns. From early, formative experiences with mountains, deserts, and the Pacific Ocean; to shaky teenage days where walking in the hills of California soothed and grounded me; to self-guided wilderness rites of passage trips with a good friend in Big Bend National Park in Texas; to being a guide on such trips with university students; and working with at-risk youth in simple garden settings. I have experienced directly the mysterious and magical ways nature supports the soul's longing and gives us exactly the medicine we need.

"While many of us humans tend to talk a lot about community, the cranes were living it. Their shrill calling was pure wildness that penetrated into our bones." "The cranes brought out a completely non-intellectual felt experience of letting otherness penetrate me. I felt myself together with them in the web of life and the great mystery."

Chapter Seven

Beyond the Human/Nature Split

To be rooted is perhaps the most important and least recognized need of the human soul.
—Simone Weil

Understanding that the human/nature split stems from unconscious beliefs that have been handed down from generation to generation helps us appreciate its deep roots and the challenges associated with healing it. The intention to reclaim a conscious and participatory relationship with the Earth guides us forward. As we open to our interbeing with soil, mountains, rivers, trees, bears, birds, and other people, our boundaries naturally soften.

Proof that the human soul is rooted in the Earth shows up in the universal experience of awe and wonder in the presence of natural beauty and in the demonstrated healing benefits of nature. As products of the full sweep of the fourteen billion year evolutionary journey of the universe, we humans are not separate from any aspect of the Earth. Through us, the universe itself has become conscious. When we look at the night sky, we are the universe looking at itself. When we find ourselves transfixed by the ocean or a sunrise, we are the Earth in awe of itself.

Our interbeing with the Earth and all beings also shows up in our pain over the degradation of the natural world and the call to action. Rainforest activist John Seed's statement, "I am part of the rainforest protecting myself" epitomizes the transformative power of this shift in consciousness.[1]

As we merge into the rhythms of the natural world, where everything exists in accordance with its true nature and essence, we align with our own essence. The ocean and wave metaphor is a good one. We arise out of the ocean of nature, out of the energetic source behind the entire universe. We take form, grow, and mature, and then dissolve back into nature. More waves, more forms take shape and dissolve in a cyclical process. As the focus on the small self, on "me" and "mine," softens, our personal problems lose at least some their significance and we can relax more.

The experience of interbeing with the natural world helps set the stage for the deeper, more radical experience of nonduality. An expanded sense of self still means that consciousness is orbiting around some sense of "me." That is not the final station on the journey toward expanded consciousness and maturity. As outlined in *The Perennial Philosophy*, human consciousness can merge with the Ground of Being itself. In this dimension we experience the unfolding of reality as a flowing unity, and all concepts of self and other—all boundaries—dissolve.

Experiencing this level of reality, we acquire a deep knowing of our essence as pure awareness and become more conscious of the life force flowing through us. A felt sense of sacredness enhances our passion for life and our care for others and the world.

In my own life, just the slightest taste of interbeing and nonduality while meditating, walking in a forest, or crying while listening to a report of people's suffering on the radio, fills me with heart-opening compassion and love. I feel how even a brief moment of this experience reorients me toward life energy itself, toward my essence as a human being, and this connects me to all of life.

I still tell myself all kinds of stories about my inadequacies and what is wrong with other people and the world, but now they are placed in a bigger context. I take myself a lot less seriously and appreciate each day and each breath much more.

Honoring Otherness

An appreciation of the nondual nature of reality does not detract from our marvelous ability as humans to discern and appreciate difference. Human development unfolds in the context of otherness—by comparisons with the life forms and other things that surround us. Some recent experiences have shown me how otherness is a kind of parallel to interbeing that adds richness and joy to life.

In March of 2014 my partner Samhitta and I went to hear a talk by local biologist Steve Jones on the sandhill crane migration. I've always had a special place in my heart for cranes, and since they would soon be moving through our area, the timing seemed right to learn more about them. In a packed auditorium Steve showed slides and played audio recordings of these birds. He told us that their spring migration was one of the greatest spectacles of nature to be found in North America.

Steve told the group about some particularly good places to experience the cranes along the Platte River in Nebraska, and Samhitta and I decided on the spot that we would go and join Steve and others there in a couple weeks, at the height of the migration. Steve's obvious love and deep connection with the cranes was contagious and helped seal the deal. Here was a man who seemed tuned into the consciousness and experience of these non-human beings. I wanted more of that ability myself and had a hunch that this trip would help.

Just before leaving for Nebraska I had an experience that shifted me. I was looking at a calendar on the wall at work. It was a nature calendar and there was a large, close-up image of the head of an emperor penguin. I looked at that picture for a long time and contemplated penguinness—penguin consciousness, priorities, and survival. Such a different way of seeing and being in the world! I felt the steadfastness and care the penguins manifest so dramatically during the harshness of the Antarctic winter. I felt the otherness of these beings in a bodily way. Rather than separate me, the appreciation of their otherness brought a sense of non-separation. Through honoring the beauty and unique qualities of penguins I was also honoring the beauty and unique qualities of every species, including my own. Otherness and interbeing came together and the world came more alive. I felt my participation with all of it in a way that brought out both tenderness and joy. I was already moving toward my longing to part the veil of separateness. I set a conscious intention to carry the momentum forward into the crane trip.

When we first arrived at the campsite Steve had described to us, we were treated to the sight of a river otter swimming in a deep pool near the small bridge we were driving over. It had been years since I had seen an otter (this was months before seeing the otters in Oregon) and Samhitta and I were thrilled. Here was another excellent opportunity to honor otherness and a most auspicious beginning to our time with the river and its wildlife.

Once the otter disappeared from sight, we noticed another vehicle in the small parking lot and saw Steve walking toward us. Steve filled us in on what the cranes were doing, telling us that they had started to arrive in small numbers and that dusk is when they were expected in the thousands. He said they usually congregate in large numbers directly across the river from where we were, and he pointed out a good place to sleep so as not to disturb them at night. We agreed to meet, along with the other people, at a particular bridge before dark.

The cranes didn't disappoint. Everyone spoke in hushed tones as we ate a potluck meal on the bridge and waited. A few birds flew over and landed a short distance upstream, then a few more. As the twilight deepened, our whispers grew louder and more excited as great flocks of cranes started to be seen on the horizon. Groups of hundreds of birds were winging their way toward us and a shallow bend in the river where they would spend the night in the relative safety of the huge congregation.

Sandhill cranes migrate in family groups and they call to each other incessantly as they navigate their way. They continue their excited conversations after landing as well, piercing the silence with the sounds of an ancient reunion—raspy, croaking voices that have reverberated in this place, what we now call Nebraska, for at least the last ten million years.[2]

While many of us humans tend to talk a lot about community, the cranes were living it. Their shrill calling was pure wildness that penetrated into our bones. I was so happy that this wildness was still in the world; that the cranes had managed to survive yet another year and find their way here. Their communion inspired my own longing to come together with others of *my* species, to communicate from a deep, wild place, and navigate the dangers ahead. I doubt that Samhitta and I were the only ones moved to tears.

And the birds kept coming. As darkness fell there were thousands gathered at select spots on the river. When we went back to the campsite we were excited to find a large flock right across the river from where we were going to sleep, just as Steve had promised. Sleeping under the stars on a clear, frosty night, listening to the cranes and watching shooting stars was a deep blessing.

We woke up to the hoo-hoo-hooting of a great horned owl and some rare quiet from the cranes. We sat up in our ice-coated sleeping bags with senses wide-awake and waited—fully connected to the quivering energy of the hundreds of cranes just across the water. As the sun topped the horizon the birds began to stir. And in much the same way they had arrived, they left. The vivacious clamor would build and a group would spring up and fly off together, then another and another, all the while calling out their passion for the day and the freedom of flight. Wave upon wave came and washed over the land. As the last flocks became faint lines on the clear horizon we sat in stunned silence, trying to take it all in. So much life, so much wildness....

After a day of feeding in the nearby fields, they would return again until they were ready to continue the journey north to Canada, Alaska, or even Siberia. We spent another day and night there and did not want to leave. We agreed that retuning to this place would be an annual ritual for us.

For weeks afterwards, Samhitta and I imitated the cranes, drew the cranes, watched videos and talked about the cranes. We celebrated them so fully they became a part of us in a conscious way. Their social nature, their voices, their tenacity, grace, and endurance—everything about them invited joyful celebration.

The cranes brought out a completely non-intellectual felt experience of letting otherness penetrate me. I felt myself together with them in the web of life and the great mystery.

The cranes changed me. Connecting with the aliveness of the cranes brings out my own aliveness. Honoring the cranes brings honor to my own life. I feel more open, humble, and compassionate. More curious about the consciousness of rocks, I slow down and become more rock-like. More open to fully experiencing mountains, trees, and rivers, I deepen my own way of being in the world. I feel saner and more grounded as a result.

With this expanded sense of interbeing and connection comes the realization that I can never fully know another—not a crane, not a tree, not a bumble bee or rock, not my lover. This deepens the sacredness of the world and helps me find and settle into my place in it.

Expanding the View of Nature and Wildness

One of the things I appreciate the most about my formal ecopsychology education was the way Naropa University put ecopsychology under the transpersonal psychology umbrella. This helped me expand my sense of interbeing to include not only the things readily considered beautiful and wild, but also, well, *everything*.

While ecopsychology is inherently a transpersonal psychology—moving beyond the personal—its transformative power is greatly magnified when it goes all the way to the Source, all the way to the Ground of Being, leaving nothing out along the way. If everything is connected and interrelated, and reality is nondual—not two—then, ultimately, it's all nature, it's all natural, it's all part of the process.

My early practices in seeing everything as nature were some of my most memorable since they challenged beliefs and values I'd held dear throughout my activist career. And since the environmental campaigner in me was still present, I had a lot of resistance towards seeing hazardous waste incinerators and coal-fired power plants as nature. It seemed a recipe for complacency and a kind of spiritual bypassing of the problems in the world. But as I let my fixed ideas soften, it made more and more sense to me that these too are expressions of life energy and the ultimate mystery that lies at the core of all things.

My full acceptance of this view is still very much a work in progress, but I know it has opened my heart. When I'm in my heart conditionally—loving some things while despising others—I'm not really in my heart at all.

One specific practice I engaged in that opened me up was sitting with a coal-fired power plant. I went with a group to the "plant" and we were invited to just be there—looking, feeling, and bearing witness. As I did this, I saw that the structure and the people associated with it were not somehow inherently evil. I saw that the people who built it and who worked there were meeting the demand for electricity, that this enterprise was a part of a whole system. Of course there were other elements as well—the profit motive and failure to account for environmental and social consequences being a couple of examples—but these didn't negate the other aspects, they only filled out the picture.

Sitting there, letting my beliefs and judgments fall away, I noticed that the building itself had its own beauty—the details in the construction and engineering, the lines of the place, the lights. I received a felt sense that because the materials themselves were of the Earth, were nature, that the building itself was also nature. It was only my thoughts, my thinking, which could make it otherwise.

Staying with the practice, I also saw into the ephemeral nature of the building, the workers, myself, and everything. This knowing that everything of the Earth will return to the Earth in due course softened my view and opened my heart.

All of which didn't magically make this industrial enterprise suddenly benign. I bore witness to the environmental and health consequences, the asthma and toxic chemical pollution. I grieved for the loons and other species impacted by the accumulation of mercury in lakes that burning coal contributes to in a significant way.

I also sat with the realization that there was so much I could not see or understand. How could one person hope to comprehend all the interconnections and ripple effects—the experience of coal miners and all the other people involved in creating this industry, the impacts to ecosystems and the whole cycle of life?

Bearing witness to this structure and process, I had many transpersonal experiences that took me beyond thinking and preferences and offered a glimpse into the infinite reality that lies beyond the personal. I got a felt sense of the interconnectedness of things and the Ground of Being itself, and there was still plenty of room for sadness and grief.

Experiences such as these have been influential moments on my path of becoming increasingly aware of who/what I really am, of the ephemeral nature of everything, and the spiritual ground that ultimately gives rise to all things. I have found that a transpersonal perspective (when I can manage it) increases my empowerment—my ability and willingness to act in the world. It's a sense of empowerment that pervades my whole life and allows for deeper feelings and expressions of love and interrelatedness.

There has also been a relaxation that comes with seeing it all as an evolutionary journey. It's a relaxation that helps me take myself less seriously and get beyond "us-versus-them" thinking. It allows me to make room for everything, even pain, uncertainty, and death. It helps me hold paradox and opens me to gratitude.

Limited concepts of what is nature and what is not, what is wild and what isn't, underestimate and devalue the raw energy that lies at the heart of existence. There are distinctions that can be made of course, and what we readily consider wilderness and open space has incalculable value in an increasingly domesticated world.

There is wholeness in what we think of as wilderness or ocean that results in innate integrity and sustainability. But just as there is no place left on Earth that remains untouched by human activity, in the end there is no final domestication either, everything is wild at its core. As domesticated as we might feel as humans, our deepest longings and the teeming billions of bacteria in our guts reveal a wild essence.

Restorative Practice
See Everything as Sacred and Impermanent

Parting the veil of separateness and seeing the truth of interbeing is the ultimate fruit of active peace and the path of restoration. Taking the time to appreciate that everything that exists in the world has arisen from the Ground of Being and has its own consciousness and energy, helps us to experience everything in the world as sacred.

When we stay mindful that everything that comes also goes, that nothing lasts forever, even mountains, dams, and oil refineries, we move more deeply into the flow of life. In this flow we can better appreciate both the beauty and the pain in the world. We can see more clearly and move more freely because we are not constrained by the ego and all its judgments about right and wrong, good and bad.

When the energy and consciousness that lies at the core of all existence is experienced as sacred, and all "things" impermanent, the whole world is re-enchanted. When we move beyond dualistic thinking and beliefs, even the pain that life brings, even the fear, even the poisonous technology, can be understood as part of the process of evolution and transformation that we are immersed in. There is a reason for everything and nothing is ever wasted.

When we practice nonattachment and not pushing anything away, we take a big step toward maturity. We practice accepting the world as it is, not because everything is wonderful, but because arguing with reality is the very root of insanity and separateness.

What follows is an exercise in seeing everything as sacred and impermanent. You will be asked to not just pick the easy things to look at, but to include those things you may not have regarded as beautiful, sacred, or even noteworthy in the past—the oil and gas drilling operation, the landfill, the neighbor or co-worker you really don't like. Not including everything sets up a duality where there is none. Dualistic thinking is just that, thinking. It is the ego's preferences and arbitrary cut between good and bad, beautiful and ugly.

Spend some time bringing mindfulness to the sacredness and impermanence of everything. Make this your meditation as you pause frequently to notice all of the people and other beings, "things," happenings, and relationships you witness and are a part of.

Decide for how long you'll do the practice. It could be half an hour, a morning or afternoon, or an entire day. However long you do it for, engage it as a practice, with energy and intention, and with gentleness and self-compassion.

Notice the little things and seemingly inconsequential events. Include the traffic light, the garbage cans, and the shopping mall. Include your own emotions and behaviors and yourself as a whole. Include everything! It's all sacred!

Practice seeing and experiencing the truth that everything and everyone arises from the same source and is ultimately spirit. If you feel that you can rule out anything as not being sacred, look deeper. Practice letting go of all attachments, preferences, and judgments.

Stay connected to your own essence, your own life energy. Use your breath to calm your mind and relax into pure being.

Don't take yourself too seriously as you engage this practice—stay loose and relaxed. Whatever your experience, notice it without any pushing away.

Notice how you feel. How does it feel to even try to see everything as sacred and impermanent? Notice if your heart is open.

When you conclude the practice, notice the quality of your mind. Notice what's just naturally there.

Creating Better Stories

We seem designed as human beings to think big and place our lives within a meaningful context. Throughout the ages, ceremony, ritual, the teachings of elders, and the myths and stories handed down through the generations facilitated the sense of place and meaning. As the life-denying worldview and the belief in separateness undermined this heritage, it eroded much of the social and cultural foundation required for healthy human development and maturity. Our stories of who we are and why we're here became disconnected from the Earth and the cosmos. They became desiccated and lifeless.

I remember being a teenager with little in the way of real elders in my life to tell me stories larger than my life in which I could situate myself. All I knew were limiting stories related to things such as how the culture measured success and how I needed to play by the rules in order to compete. I learned that being a "good boy" was the most important thing; certainly also the message that God was outside of myself and *that*, of course, was a perfect fit with messages that I wasn't good enough and worthy of love. It was quite a set up and I continue to feel the effects of it every day.

Peacemakers need the support of healthy stories that bring us more fully alive. The good news, since we are essentially filling a vacuum, is that we can use everything we know and feel in creating new stories that fit our times and our experience.

We have vast bodies of wisdom we can tap: ancient wisdom from indigenous peoples and the wisdom of the spiritual traditions, as well as the more recent understandings stemming from the sciences. We can synthesize and integrate this wisdom—cross-pollinating to create and *be* living examples of consciousness that have never existed before.

The great stories now being called forth interweave our human existence with the greater tapestry of Earth and cosmos—they embed us fully in the material world *and* recognize and celebrate our spiritual essence. They shift us from isolation to interconnection, from individualism to collective co-creation. They help us hold paradox and invite us into the felt sense of interbeing.

Part of the story I now tell includes a personal account of how my wounds helped me survive and created a personality structure that I am learning to embrace and even love. Trying to cast out certain traits or parts of myself hasn't worked so well, so for me, it's now all about allowing—making peace with what is and honoring it all as sacred. Self-awareness and self-acceptance have become touchstones and close allies. This puts me in a much better position to value my needs and stand-up for them when necessary.

My story also includes a deep knowing that after only three days out on the land camping, my civilized self shakes loose and my connection to and longing for the Earth finds me. I remember who I am. I remember that the Earth is my larger body. Despite the ease and comfort of civilized life, the wildness at my core is truer, more intimate and resonant—like comparing punk rock to a soulful folk ballad.

If we are to survive and live into mutually-enhancing ways to be with the Earth, we will need some damn good stories that we believe with every cell in our bodies to help inspire and guide us.

And since this book is ultimately aimed at cultivating the experience of the transpersonal, it's worth saying again and as clearly as possible, that any story worthy of our time and our evolutionary journey will support us in our spiritual maturity. If there is one thing that will save us, it's the deep embrace of our spiritual essence—the lived experience of interbeing and oneness that dissolves the boundaries and makes peace possible.

Similar to the way that mindfulness isn't just a nice idea, but the very foundation for showing up in the world as mature adults, working with the human/nature split is an absolute necessity for our survival as a species. Participation and reciprocity form the basis for a new way of being that brings us home and catalyzes our healing.

For most of us, recovering from the human/nature split will be a long-term process. As we consciously deepen our participation and practice reciprocity we'll be able to feel the support of the Earth more and more profoundly. We can honor and celebrate more joyfully the non-human beings we share this planet with—relatives who offer us beauty and companionship and exemplify wholeness, integrity, and resilience; who know who they are and how to live gracefully in the places they inhabit.

Every time we respond to any experience with the awareness of interbeing we contribute toward creating a new story. Every time we feel the Earth as our larger body, we expand and evolve our consciousness. Every conscious act ripples out and affects the whole world.

"I was participating in a weeklong workshop and re-treat...practicing staying right in the present moment, noticing my internal experiences while I was with other people. I sensed how opening to the longing to connect with other people, and feeling safe enough to follow that longing, made room for the whole world to enter."

Chapter Eight

Restoring Our
Interpersonal Relationships

If you want to go quickly, go alone.
If you want to go far, go together.
—African proverb

Relationship is the thread that most profoundly interweaves my view of restoration. As I've explored the territory of change at the personal and societal levels, the path never fails to circle back to relationship: the ongoing work of coming into healthy relationship with myself, other people, other species, the Earth, and spirit.

Like the early ecologists pointing out the importance of the web of relationships within ecosystems, research is finding that healthy interpersonal relationships are essential to our mental, emotional, and physical health. The relationship needs so basic to our survival as children carry forward into adulthood and are increasingly vital to our survival as a species.

Building on the Foundations

Building a strong foundation for interpersonal relationships through mindfulness and transpersonal awareness is key because when we show up for *any* relationship stuck in immature patterns, we are practically assured to make a mess of things. Meaningful and rich relations with other people invariably stretch us and challenge our egos. While these challenges may feel uncomfortable in the moment, in the end they are blessings that create opportunities for growth and transformation.

When we cultivate an open awareness that moves us beyond simplistic judgments about other people, the walls of separation begin to crumble. In the present moment there is no story, there is only the truth of our interrelatedness and shared humanity.

The mediation and coaching work I do always begins with mindfulness. Without grounding in the present moment, it is almost impossible to shift out of damaging patterns of thinking and behavior. Dropping the external focus on other people and events helps us feel into our own experience. When we do that, we break the spell that strong emotions such as anger, resentment, and feeling like a victim can cast over us.

Mindfulness focused on what is happening in the body opens the door to the direct experience of our interrelatedness with the natural world and other people. Engaging in interpersonal relationships from this place, we become more stable and find a longing for communion and intimacy that flows not from neediness and a sense of lack, but from fullness and health.

The Need for Training and Tools

With the foundations of mindfulness and nature-based practices, we are ready to enter the challenging territory of interpersonal relationships with greater awareness and resilience.

We need the foundations because despite being hardwired for relationship, most of us have received little in the way of training and tools that support openness, respectful communication, and conflict resolution.

Without the support of skills and practices, we easily lose our center as soon as conflict arises. One moment we are an adult having an adult conversation, and in the next we are four years old and wanting to take our toys and go home. Growth always takes place at the edge of our comfort zone and nothing forces us to grow up as much as interpersonal relationships.

When I first came across the kinds of tools and teachings I'll be presenting here, I was in my mid-forties. I felt like a desert wanderer who, on the verge of death, came upon a source of beautiful clear water. I was recently divorced and grieving my inability to work through the conflicts in the marriage. The marriage challenges were just the tip of the relationship iceberg that had weighed me down my entire adult life.

The life-denying worldview based on separateness couldn't care less about relationships. Knowing who we are, where we are, why we are here, and how to get along better is not a priority. In fact, such understanding is a serious threat to business as usual, far more dangerous than any band of armed revolutionaries could ever hope to be.

The isolation and insecurity the belief in separateness instills leads to an attitude of scarcity and competition—"I'm not enough and there isn't enough to go around, so I'm going to get as much as I can." This view leads to more insecurity and isolation as a vicious cycle is perpetuated. Not exactly the ingredients for healthy relationships.

Active Peace beckons us toward something quite different. A life-affirming worldview recognizes the truth of interrelatedness and puts a high priority on relationships at every level. More than any technological fix, more than any new, inspired leader, we need to learn how to get along better.

Before delving into some of the nuts and bolts of creating healthier and more satisfying relationships, I want to share a personal story that speaks to the importance of interpersonal relationships and the foundations presented thus far in this book. I referred to this story earlier as a direct experience of interbeing; it was also a profound experience of dropping into my essence and the felt sense of life energy moving through me.

I was participating in a weeklong workshop and retreat, and for several days we'd been practicing staying right in the present moment, noticing our internal experiences while we were with other people.

As I worked with my awareness in this subtle way, I noticed how with each moment, each "now," there was indeed something new and fresh to experience. I also noticed that as the practice continued, I was left feeling more alive and awake than ever before.

During some time designated for silence and integration, I found a soft, dry place to sit at the base of a large cedar tree. As I sat with my back to the tree, feeling the support of the tree and the Earth, I looked out at the forest. A very deep relaxation washed over me and all of a sudden I *was* awareness itself.

I felt myself moving between two different states of consciousness. One was the pure awareness that transcended all longing and sense of "me." The other was a soft and open sense of self, and in that consciousness I felt the life energy at the core of my being. I was aware of the vibrancy of the energy and how it wasn't mine at all—it was life expressing itself through me.

As I sat there rapt in the mystery, I became aware of the longing in the life energy. I noticed a longing for expression and flow, a longing to be fully and wildly alive. There was a longing to merge with the world—the sunlight, the green of the leaves, the bird song, and the people. The people? This was one of the most surprising and delicious aspects of the experience.

The longing to merge with nature was familiar territory for me. But such a deep longing to connect with other people transcended my usual lone wolf tendencies. What happened after I went back into the group brought more surprises.

From then on, as I sat with another person, I could feel a deep longing for connection with her or him and all the people in the room. In that longing was a desire to be free and open, to be completely uncensored and uninhibited, to play and be joyous and be the animals we are.

I began to get a felt sense of the connections that were already there in the relational field. With each person there was a sense of presence and interbeing. I felt how, sitting with one person, the energy of all the interconnections of all the people in the room was right there too. And this wasn't limited to the people.

Without any kind of effort, sitting across from another person and looking at her, I could feel the presence of the forest that surrounded us. The birds, otters, and other animals I had seen earlier—all of it was present right then and there in an energetic way. Extending from that was the realization that everything—the world itself and the universe—was present then and in any given moment.

I went on to feel how such an understanding imbues the present moment with rich potential to live from the truth of interbeing. It was also clear that the restorative practices I had engaged in up until that time had laid the groundwork. Most specifically and surprisingly, I sensed how opening to the longing to connect with other people, and feeling safe enough to follow that longing, made room for the whole world to enter.

"*Restorative practice gives us a foundation for explor-ing a completely different way of communicating with others. We can keep our relationships fresh and alive, address issues as they arise, and not get loaded down by emotional baggage.*"

Chapter Nine

Relationship Skills and Tools

The more we give our best, the more we are able to receive other people's worst. Isn't that great?

— Chögyam Trungpa

With the health and resilience that comes through the foundations of mindfulness and nature-based practices, we can back up our longing for relationship with action. We cultivate clarity, relaxation, and groundedness. We know we will often not get just what we want, that we will be challenged, yet we also have new capacities to meet the interpersonal needs that go so much deeper than the ego. With nowhere to hide, with our vulnerability and integrity leading the way, we meet in the open field of our shared humanity to do the work of ending war in our hearts and minds, in our interpersonal relationships and, ultimately, in our societies and the world.

Once again, intention is a good place to start. We don't have to have everything all figured out. We don't need to engrave our stories and our wounds in stone and get every detail right! We don't need to understand other people completely—or at all! What we most need to be in relationships as adults is to know how *we* want to show up right *now*! The unconscious mind is simple and it responds to simple, clear instructions. Those instructions are your intention.

Restorative Practice
Intention Setting

Bring to mind a relationship that can sometimes or often be difficult. Imagine that you are about to engage in a challenging dialogue with this person. Notice the sensations, thoughts, feelings, and emotions that arise.

Use your breath to quiet your mind and let your awareness drop into your body.

With each inhale take in more relaxation, with each exhale release more tension.

When you feel ready, check in with yourself in an honest way:

Is your heart open as you imagine having this dialogue?

Can you see who this other person is beyond the thoughts and story you have about him or her?

What are you really longing for in this relationship?

Can you move out of a protected state of consciousness and into vulnerability?

Are you prepared to set an intention that prioritizes this relationship and acknowledges the interrelatedness of everything?

Set an intention that works for you in this situation. Your intention may be simply to stay present to your own experience, or to listen in an open way. You don't have to pretend to be Gandhi or the Buddha or anything you are not.

When the opportunity arises to actually have this or a similar dialogue, let your intention guide you by simply holding it in your awareness.

Feelings, Needs, and the Deep Longing

Nothing has proven more valuable to me than bringing awareness to the feelings, needs, and deep longings present in relationships. As I related in the preface of this book, it was not very long ago that I had very little conscious awareness of what I was feeling in my body. I didn't know how to distinguish between feelings and emotions. I had little understanding of and appreciation for the universal needs of human beings, and had no clue what my deep longings were.

Helping people begin to explore their feelings using the basics of "angry, happy, sad, afraid," is a common entry point. Yet even in this simple example we see the failure to distinguish between feelings and emotions, between what can be felt in the body and what is based on thinking. I have found it so helpful to make this distinction.

The alternative to declaring "I'm angry," and responding in a habitual way, is to go inside and feel the shakiness, the holding in the belly, the tightness in the chest. Instead of getting lost in a train of thoughts, if we can stay connected to ourselves and to what's happening in our bodies, we can stay conscious and aware. This allows us to stay in our integrity and stay connected to other people, regardless of what we are feeling.

Feelings that can be felt in the body include, but are in no way limited to: shaky, constricted, cool, cold, warm, hot, jittery, achy, tight, nervous, loose, ease, comfort, discomfort, pain, arousal, agitation, quiet, expanded, deflated, shut down, pumped up, nervous, panic, anxious, connected, disconnected, distress, irritation, relaxation, clarity, calm, upset, settled, unsettled, scared, terror, restless, tired, rested, energized, joyful, centered, frazzled, overwhelmed, grounded, ungrounded, open, and closed.

Needs are important because they influence everything we do. If we track our experience closely enough we find that our feelings are always linked to basic human needs that are either being met or not being met in the moment. For example, when I find myself feeling nervous before speaking in a large group, I know that needs for acceptance, understanding, and connection are in play. After speaking, I may still feel shaky and nervous because I'm still longing for these needs to be met, or I may feel some ease and openness due to a sense of having been heard and understood.

Life energy moves through us and expresses itself as universal human needs that include acceptance, belonging, connection, companionship, understanding, intimacy, sexual expression, respect, appreciation, safety, peace, autonomy, freedom, ease, play, meaning, purpose, and needs related to physical survival and health such as air, water, food, and shelter.

In his book, *Nonviolent Communication: A Language of Life,* Marshall Rosenberg writes:

> Judgments, criticisms, diagnoses, and interpretations of others are all alienated expressions of our own unmet needs. If someone says, "You never understand me," they are really telling us that their need to be understood is not being fulfilled. If a wife says, "You've been working late every night this week; you love your work more than you love me," she is saying that her need for intimacy is not being met.[1]

In my work as a mediator, relationship coach, and youth mentor, I have found that the most basic step is to bring awareness to the feelings and needs that are unconsciously directing behavior and emotions. For example, the simple act of naming the feelings and needs I heard expressed in someone's story, never fails to help them feel heard and understood. "Sounds like you're really angry and frustrated. I'm guessing you'd like to feel more respected?" Hearing their feelings and needs named calms people down and opens up the space where healing can happen.

The ability to track the felt sense of feelings and needs connects us to life energy itself. This is the ground from which we can connect to others in an authentic way.

What am I feeling in my body right now? What am I needing? What can I do that will help meet my need? Is there a request I can make of this other person that will help meet my need and deepen our connection? What is he feeling and needing? Simple questions such as these go far in creating the kind of environment where relationships can be restored, deepened, and sustained.[2]

Here's an example that puts feelings and needs together with a clear request: "I feel scared when you drive this fast and I'd really like to feel more relaxed and safe right now. Would you be willing to drive the speed limit?" Compare that communication with something that's perhaps a bit more typical: "Slow Down!" It's pretty hard to argue with the first statement because the speaker is simply speaking her truth and the request *is* a request and not a demand. The driver may or may not be willing to slow down but there isn't an argument. On the other hand, "Slow Down!" pretty much assures either argument or resentment or both.

Underneath the many needs in play in our most meaningful relationships, there are deep longings that most clearly represent the life force in action. For me this seems to show up most consistently as a longing for connection, but not just any kind of connection. There is a longing for connection with other people that is infinitely expansive, where the boundaries disappear, the acceptance total, the freedom complete.

I've noticed that paying attention to the deep longing keeps me curious and awake to the life energy that lives in me and seeks engagement and intimacy with the world. It's a relationship energy that has been stifled for a very long time. Simply bringing awareness to this energy has changed my capacity for all sorts of relationships, including my relationship to life itself.

Restorative Practice
Connect with Life Energy and the Deep Longing[3]

This is a practice for exercising the ability to tune into life energy and the deep longing you may have in relation to another person. This capacity opens the door, not only to much more soulful relationships, but to the transformational energy needed to create a healthier world.

Bring to mind someone you care about and have a relationship with. Imagine that you are sitting in front of her or him.

Use your breath to quiet your mind and let your awareness drop deep into your body. Really take your time and let your awareness settle.

When you feel ready, ask yourself, "What is alive in me right now as I imagine sitting with this person?" "What feelings and needs am I aware of?"

Stay with these questions and avoid falling into patterns of judgment and thinking. Stay with your breath and body. Name the feelings and needs for yourself.

Once the feelings and needs are very present, tune into them as life energy. Notice how the energy at the core of your existence is right now manifesting through you as these feelings and longings.

From this place of presence and openness, ask yourself, "What is the deep longing I have with this person?" "What is my life energy longing for in and through this relationship?" There may be a longing for expression, communion, flow, and fullness. Just notice what you notice. No right way, no wrong way.

Move back and forth between bringing awareness to the longing itself and feeling the life energy in the longing. This is deep awareness practice; take your time and be gentle with yourself.

As you wind down the exercise, ask yourself, "What will I carry forward from this exercise into this relationship?" "What is worth remembering here?"

Regardless of what comes up, honor it as your truth. Take some time to celebrate the amazing ability to feel deeply. Celebrate even the simple desire to feel deeply.

Understanding Triggers

Despite our best intentions, we often get overtaken by strong emotional responses and lose the connection to other people. Often referred to as being triggered, some people prefer the term "restimulated." The concept of restimulation is useful in understanding triggers because it makes it clear that when we find ourselves taken over by an emotional state, it usually means an experience from when we were young has been touched.

The actual triggers are external events such as words, tones of voice, and behaviors that instantaneously create an emotional response in us. When triggered, we shift into automatic pilot and go unconscious to a certain extent.

We can see this most clearly in hindsight when we notice how disproportional our response was to a particular stimulus. For example, all he did was walk by without saying hello and I immediately judged him as an uncaring spacecase who has no respect for me.

When we are triggered, the rational neocortex goes off-line and the limbic system runs the show. The limbic system's faster and more primitive operation helps explain the feelings of being overwhelmed and the defensiveness that arise when we are triggered. We respond in irrational ways because defensiveness trumps relationship building in the heat of the moment.

Common signs of being triggered[4] include:

- Physical signs—not breathing or breathing fast, rapid heart rate, muscle tension, and shakiness;

- Thinking signs—blaming, justifying, and resentful thoughts, thoughts of revenge, and obsessively repeating judgments and other thoughts;

- Emotional signs—feelings of anger, hatred, or fear; feeling shut down, feeling like a victim, feeling checked out or like you just want to go to sleep; and

- Behavioral signs—saying things you don't mean, using insults, sarcasm, and blame; screaming, yelling, door slamming, running away and other forms of isolating, talking faster than normal, or refusing to communicate at all.

When we are triggered, our vision narrows and we disconnect from the whole person we are dealing with. We lose touch with her basic goodness as well as our own. Along the way, we also lose track of what was actually said or done. Instead, we make assumptions and judgments and draw conclusions. Our core beliefs about ourselves, other people, and the world will write the script for what we project onto this other person or situation.

This is altogether human and not bad news at all. Our triggers give us the basic information we need to continue our healing. Following the clues leads us right into the depth of our wounds and deepest longings. If we dare to explore this territory we will find greater self-understanding and acceptance. We will continue to get triggered of course—it comes with the package—but our learning and practice will rewire the brain and we will find ourselves more relaxed and able to handle any situation.

I have noticed that working with my triggers has, over time, reduced the frequency, duration, and intensity of my emotional responses. This work has increased my self-acceptance and humility and, as a consequence, I'm more accepting and less judgmental of others.

Restorative Practice
Know Your Triggers

Find a time and a quiet place to be still and practice mindfulness. When you feel ready, recall a recent situation that triggered you and respond to the following questions:

What was the trigger or stimulus?

What happened in your body? What were the physical sensations?

What thoughts and feelings arose?

What are the unmet needs or longings that lay underneath the response?

Can you bring empathy and acceptance to the unmet needs and how you responded?

Can you feel the life energy at the root of the longing?

Work with these questions using a couple of past situations and then start to work with them in new situations, right in the moment or as soon after the stimulus as you can.

Resourcing Ourselves

The flip side of what triggers us is the way we calm ourselves down and stay grounded. For example, we may have discovered that taking a walk, or talking things out with a friend helps us come back to our center. It can be helpful to bring even more consciousness to the ways we "resource" ourselves so that these approaches can become more effective and habitual. It can also be helpful to consider and strengthen resource areas we may be underutilizing. Categories of such resources include:

Psychological – A healthy sense of self; access to self-awareness and a full range of feelings and emotions; appreciation of challenges and humor; a felt sense of meaning, purpose, and contribution;

Relational – A felt sense of deserving and having friendship and support;

Spiritual – A felt sense of connection to source/God/spirit;

Physical – A felt sense of good health and vitality;

Sensual – A felt sense of pleasure from all of the senses;

Intellectual – A felt sense of the ability to think things through, to see patterns, to be interested and curious;

Artistic/Creative – A felt sense of having outlets for inspiration and expression; and

Nature – A felt sense of interconnectedness with the Earth and other species; a felt sense of support, inspiration, and care.

I emphasize the felt sense in these examples because that is what makes them resources and not just concepts. We can feel the fullness of the support of these resources when we slow down and really notice how certain activities contribute to our lives.

In this supported place, we can better notice the way that destructive thoughts and strong emotions come, stir up a little trouble and then vanish. They may create a few ripples on the surface of the lake, but underneath the surface, the water is calm and still. Along with the practices comes greater confidence and capacity to operate outside of our comfort zones—we can trust that we'll be okay, that we can calm and ground ourselves even after the most challenging interactions.

Examples of practices in each resource area include:

Psychological – Positive self-talk, psychotherapy, mindfulness practices, journaling, conscious relationship building, volunteer/service work, time in nature, rites of passage, and play;

Relational – Sharing from the heart with friends, writing to or calling a friend, visiting family, relationship/family counseling, using communication skills, and participating in men's/women's groups;

Spiritual – Prayer, meditation, reading or listening to spiritual teachings, yoga and t'ai chi, time in nature, connecting with your sense of purpose, silence, and regular expressions of gratitude and appreciation;

Physical – Conscious breathing, walking, hiking, biking, swimming, jogging, yoga, weight lifting, martial arts, massage, dancing, and rest;

Sensual – Bringing more awareness to the senses, mindful eating and walking, sacred sexuality, massage, skinny dipping, and sunbathing;

Intellectual – Studying, writing, taking classes, learning a foreign language, and professional development;

Artistic/Creative – Journaling, drama/acting, playing music, painting, photography, and writing and reading poetry; and

Nature – Nature-based mindfulness practices, hiking, building relationships with non-human beings, tree-hugging, dirt-worshipping, and wilderness-based rites of passage.

Noticing Judgments

The highest form of human intelligence is the ability to observe without making judgments.
—Krishnamurti

Our tendency when triggered is to lose touch with the present moment and what is actually happening. With narrowed vision, and in an automatic and rapid-fire way, we make a judgment and act based on limited information.

Here is a very simple example of this process in action. Let's say it's your first day at a new job. The executive director of the organization, whom you met briefly the day you interviewed, approaches you. You hope and expect that she will stop and say hi and offer you a warm welcome. Instead, she gives you a quick glance, and without a smile or hello continues on into her office and shuts the door behind her. Your immediate, automatic response will likely be to take it personally at some level and conclude that she is cold, uninterested in you, and will be no fun at all to work with.

Your judgment about her is strong and has a kind of finality to it. For the moment at least, you have cast her in stone as uncaring and already there is strain and tension in the relationship. Maybe next time you see her you will choose to ignore her altogether.

Now consider how very little information this judgment was based on. Everything that was going on in her life, and had nothing to do with you, got left out of the equation. What if, instead of taking it personally, you just stayed open? You probably know from your own experience, how often first impressions and judgments don't hold up over time, how limited and limiting they are.

Making judgments about other people is so second nature we rarely give them a moment's reflection. So the first step is to simply notice them and relax our grip. When held loosely, we can step back from the judgment and bring awareness and curiosity to our own experience—what we are thinking, feeling, and wanting.

Recognizing and naming judgments as judgments keeps them from solidifying into more absolute kinds of beliefs about who someone else is. When held loosely, judgments can be seen as just a part of what the brain does and will be much less likely to do any real damage. When they stay unconscious, however, and are mistaken for truth, they can easily cause harm and damage relationships.

Our judgments really, *really*, don't have anything to do with anyone else! When I make a judgment about somebody, *I create* a problem and make it about him. I lose touch with myself *and* him. I'm not taking self-responsibility and I'm caught in the illusion of separateness.

The Drama Triangle

The Drama Triangle[5] highlights the habitual roles we often take in relationships when in conflict or involved in some other form of drama. It helps us identify not only when we're triggered and how we're responding, but also what may lie underneath habitual responses.

Persecutor   **Rescuer**

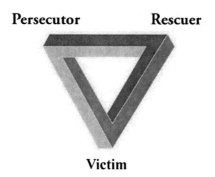

Victim

The Persecutor

The persecutor takes an angry and critical attack-mode position; controls through fear and intimidation, and may say or feel things like, "You're wrong!" Fear and feeling threatened can bring out the persecutor.

The Victim

The victim takes an overtly disempowered position; controls with blame and guilt and may say or feel things like, "Look what you did to me!" Fear that triggers feelings of helplessness, resignation, and shame can bring out the victim.

The Rescuer

The rescuer takes a "fixer" position; controls through trying to help, whether it's wanted or not, and may say or feel things like, "I know what to do. Let me help you." Fear that triggers feelings of guilt, insecurity, and shame can bring out the rescuer.

One of the key features of the Drama Triangle is the tendency to jump from role to role. Persecutors can become victims if they feel everyone is ganging up on them. Or they might accept blame, feel guilty, and become rescuers. Victims can build up so much repressed anger they become persecutors, and when that doesn't work out, rescuers. Rescuers can become victims or persecutors if not allowed to help.

All of the positions on the Drama Triangle are ultimately fueled by fear, insecurity, and lack of self-awareness. When we are on the Triangle we sacrifice our power by living in the past and being caught up in our thoughts. Noticing and understanding the roles we take helps us get off the Drama Triangle and come into our adult selves.

Restorative Practice
Use the Drama Triangle

List some recent examples from your own life of being on the Drama Triangle.

What position do you tend to take on the Triangle when triggered?

Are there examples you can think of where you moved from one role to another?

What thoughts are associated with each position?

What would happen in these situations if, instead of taking a position on the Triangle, you took 100% responsibility for your experience—for your thoughts, feelings, needs, emotions, and behaviors?

Restorative Communication

When we are in touch with our longing for connection, we naturally want to communicate in a way that is true to that longing. Restorative practice gives us a foundation for exploring a completely different way of communicating with others. We can keep our relationships fresh and alive, address issues as they arise and not get loaded down by emotional baggage.

Empathy and Deep Listening
A focus on feelings and needs helps ground your communication in empathy and deep listening. Empathy is the gentle,

non-judgmental understanding and appreciation of your own experience and the experience of others. We can think of it as pure presence, as being with yourself or another with full attention and awareness.

Empathy is a deep skill because, when pain is involved, we tend to want to jump to either avoidance or problem solving based on our fear of pain and discomfort.

Even when we start with empathy, staying with it takes mindfulness and commitment. We might have the best intentions to stay vulnerable and empathetic with someone, only to find that when they respond in a certain way we shut down. We may start out consciously listening for their feelings and needs, but after shutting down the only things we notice are our own judgments, resentments, and other thoughts.

Practicing self-empathy is good training for developing empathy toward others. We bring awareness to our feelings and the unmet needs underlying the feelings. We offer understanding and appreciation for the reasons why we are thinking and feeling as we are. This opens the heart and expands our self-acceptance.

Deep listening is a natural outgrowth of empathy, of wanting to know what is really going on with other people. While it may sound quite simple, deep listening is also a skill that takes practice to develop; hearing is automatic and passive, listening is active.

Deep listening with a focus on the underlying needs of the speaker helps us hear what is actually being said instead of getting lost in our own judgments and conclusions about what they are saying. For example, if someone says to you while you are driving, "Cutting in front of that driver so close was really stupid," your automatic response would probably be to take it personally and get defensive, "You're crazy, there was plenty of room!"

The deep listening and more empathic alternative would be to listen for the underlying needs, and then say something like, "Okay, I hear that you want to feel safe. I'll be more careful." Can you feel the difference in the quality of the connection? In the first example, the original speaker is left feeling almost completely unheard. In the latter, that person will feel heard, understood, and respected.

Empathy and deep listening fit perfectly with staying connected to our own experience and support two-way communication. For example, if someone says to you, "That was a stupid thing to do," you can stay with what was actually said and how it made you feel. Instead of getting defensive, you can simply let them know how it made you feel: "When you said that to me, it made me feel like *I* was stupid. I know that's not what you said, but I'm feeling kind of shaky and not very connected to you right now."

This way of speaking may seem awkward and unrealistic, but notice how it keeps you in self-responsibility, and remember, it's a practice, a way of bringing more life to relationships. While it may not be what you're used to, try it and see how it feels. If what you say is honest and comes from the heart, it will probably feel more satisfying than the more typical, superficial way of communicating. Being really listened to and feeling heard is a rare gift in our culture.

I recall being in a training and getting very triggered by one of the facilitators. I had wanted to speak in the group but felt completely shut down by her. At the break, one of the participants approached me and asked me "how I was feeling" with such empathy and presence that my eyes filled with tears. I cried not because I was so upset, but because her care and the quality of our connection in that moment touched me so deeply. I was obviously in a vulnerable place and had a longing to be seen and understood. With a bare minimum of words we shared a profound communication.

Mindful Speech

Bringing mindfulness to everything we say is another potent practice. What the Buddhists call "right speech," is mindful speech that is "free of lying, gossip, exaggeration, harsh language, and foolish babble."[6] Mindful speech also recognizes that the space between the words is as important as the words themselves.

Mindful speech includes the avoidance of words that do not promote relationship building. Marshall Rosenberg pointed out that words and phrases such as "should," "must," and "have to," along with labeling people as "good" and "bad," goes hand in hand with violence.[7]

Words like *should* and *must* ignore our freedom of choice and contribute to blind obedience. Labels such as *good* and *bad* tend to be judgments based on our own perspectives and do not represent the truth.

With mindful speech we are simple and real, not trying to build ourselves up or bring others down. This significantly thins out the words we use and creates much more silence, relaxation, and space. In that space, empathy and deep listening are possible.

One of the ways I've found to practice mindful speech is to notice when I'm about to say something about someone that I would not say directly to his or her face. I've noticed how this practice creates ease in me because I know I am not sowing seeds of conflict and resentment. Another practice that I've found helpful is to simply allow room for a pause before taking my turn to speak and using that time to notice what I am feeling and wanting in the moment.

I'm still learning to use these tools and accept the fact that things don't always work out the way I would like; I still sometimes make a mess of things and find myself not feeling good about myself and others. But now, unlike in the past, I have the ability to own my part and clean things up, and that has proven to be one the most powerful interpersonal practices of all.

Scott welcomes a participant back to base camp
after a 3-day wilderness solo

"Like travelers in unfamiliar territory, it can be helpful to have a map to help us navigate interpersonal relationships. All of our tools and resources are more helpful when we are clear on how we want to live our lives and treat other people."

Transforming Conflict

Everything presented in this book thus far can help us understand and transform conflict. The strong emotions so often associated with conflict such as anger, sadness, and grief serve the important role of informing us when our needs are not being met. They aren't good or bad, they are simply indicators that our life energy is seeking some kind of movement. The Latin root of the word *emotion* is "to move." We can think of feelings as actual sensations we feel in our bodies, and emotions as thoughts that create their own energy.

The conflict that so naturally arises in relationship is yet more proof that we are all connected. Conflict helps us learn about who we are and what we need. We practice making boundaries that keep us safe and in our integrity. We practice being truthful and authentic. When navigated consciously, conflict leads to deeper and more resilient relationships.

Here again it is helpful to remember that we are not our thoughts, even those strong ones that seem to take us over so completely. As with other thoughts, anger, fear, and grief arise of their own volition, not because we willed them into existence. So it is not *my* anger, it is just the energy of anger expressing, in a kind of backhanded way, a deeper longing.

If instead of attaching to the angry thoughts, I go into the body and attend to the longing—maybe a longing for understanding, connection, or ease—the energy will quickly shift. Attending to my own experience, I open up my awareness and am once again available for relationship. Self-awareness and self-acceptance lay the foundation for transforming conflict into truth telling and deeper understanding; instead of running away, we immerse ourselves in interbeing.

Chapter Ten

Restorative Practice
Transforming Strong Emotions

Connecting in a conscious way to the unmet needs and longings that give rise to strong emotions transforms the energy into compassion and brings us more alive.

Choose an interpersonal relationship that is challenging and often leads to a sense of being triggered. This can include grief and sadness related to the loss of someone you love. Bring this person to mind along with some of the situations that caused you pain.

Notice the judgments and other thoughts that arise in response to the discomfort. These may be judgments and thoughts about yourself or the other person. Notice any tendency to censor these thoughts and resist the temptation; just let them flow and feel their energy.

Once you can really feel the energy of the emotions, take some deep conscious breaths. Bring your awareness fully into your body, let the thoughts go, and feel your feelings—the actual sensations in your body. Notice the feelings that are present without judging or analyzing them.

Underneath the feelings there are unmet needs. Let conscious breathing help you stay with the body while you feel into the needs that are present. What is it you are longing for in your relationship with this person?

Feel the life energy this longing represents. Like a river reaching for the ocean, your life energy moves toward wholeness. However it feels, don't resist the energy that is present, harvest it for more clarity and aliveness.

Relax into this energy and notice its quality. Notice the quality of your mind, your awareness, as you do this.

> *Once you feel well connected with the longing that is present, give yourself some empathy—after all, you are just trying to feel safe, happy, and whole; you are just trying to meet basic universal human needs.*
>
> *Stay with the body and notice any shifts that have happened. Notice the felt sense of simple aliveness. How would it be to connect with other people from this place of presence?*

Restorative Justice

What about repairing the harm that so regularly happens in interpersonal relationships or groups? What about healing relationships that have been severely damaged through crime or other forms of serious harm? In such situations, how can we seek both justice and the restoration of relationships? Regardless of the specifics and degree of harm, the practices and principles of restorative justice offer guidance in bringing people and relationships back into balance.

Imagine that a crime has taken place. Imagine that instead of a courtroom scenario, the person who caused the harm and his support people are sitting in a circle with those who were harmed and their support people. People representing the community are present, as is the arresting officer. Two people are there to facilitate the process. Ground rules based on respect are agreed upon. One person will speak at a time without being interrupted. There will be time to say what needs to be said.

The person who caused the harm begins by telling the group what he did—what he was thinking, feeling, and needing at the time of the offense, and what he believes the harm to be. Those harmed then speak directly to the offender about what the harm actually was—how his actions have impacted their lives and made them feel. Others in the circle get their turn to speak to the harm from their perspectives. All of the many ways the harm rippled out to impact the victims and the community are named. After hearing all this, the person who caused the harm tells the group how he feels about what he did now and, looking each person in the eyes, takes responsibility for the harm he caused.

The circle then addresses what needs to happen to repair the harm. The offender starts by saying what he is willing to do. Others add their views and the facilitators help the group work through to a consensus. Everyone agrees that if the person who caused the harm does the specific things agreed upon within a certain timeframe, the harm will have been repaired and a fresh start will be possible without lingering shame, blame, and resentment. This is restorative justice in action.

It's not the easy way out for people who have caused harm. I have seen how difficult it is for offenders to look those who were harmed in the eyes and take responsibility with no excuses. In return, victims benefit from hearing directly from offenders what they were thinking, why they did what they did, what they are struggling with, and seeing other aspects of who they are. There is also the peace of mind of knowing that because of the process, it is much less likely that reoffending will occur.

The Five Rs of Restorative Justice

The five Rs of restorative justice—responsibility, respect, relationship, repair, and reintegration—reflect the heart and soul of the work and form an outline for the process. Each "R" sets a certain intention but there are also logical questions that flow from each one. I have found that these questions can easily be tailored to most any situation.

Responsibility – What happened? What was the harm that resulted? Who was harmed and how? What are the ripple effects of the harm? How was the community harmed?

What were the people (or person) who caused the harm thinking? Why did they do it? What were the needs underlying the behavior? What do the people who caused the harm take responsibility for? How do they feel about what they did now? What, if anything, needs to be done to encourage more responsibility?

Respect – Is respect being offered to everyone involved, including self-respect? What are the strengths of the people who caused the harm? What does respect look like? What limits respect? What, if anything, needs to be done to encourage more respect?

Relationship – Who are the primary support people for those most directly involved? What other relationships are important? What are some of the satisfying qualities found in these relationships? How have these relationships been harmed by the behavior in question?

Repair – What has been done to repair the harm? Do the people who were harmed feel restored? Have the ripple effects of the harm been addressed and repaired? Have the relationships been restored? Has the harm to the community been repaired? Do the people who caused the harm feel restored? Is there more that needs to be done to repair the harm and, if so, what are some specific actions that can be taken?

Reintegration – Once the harm has been repaired, is everyone involved willing to allow full reintegration of the people who caused the harm back into the community without shame or guilt? What does success/getting back to normal look like in this situation? Are the coping skills of those involved strong enough to support their wellbeing and success? What kinds of additional support would be helpful?

This is what justice looks like beyond the illusion of separateness. In the last chapter we will look at how the questions flowing from the five Rs could be used in a restorative process to repair the harm caused by British Petroleum's huge oil spill in the Gulf of Mexico.

I've used restorative justice in a variety of contexts and have yet to find a situation where the five Rs could not be tailored to the situation. I have found it satisfying to bring restorative justice into my work with youth who are in the criminal justice system, soon to be released, but still in need of restoration. I've also found restorative justice principles very helpful in mediation and relationship coaching.

The full flowering of restorative justice will take it well beyond the confines of the criminal justice system. It is already used in many schools, and its continued spread into families, neighborhoods, and organizations will change who we are in fundamental ways. Employing the principles in a day-to-day manner builds the emotional intelligence and empathy needed to avoid harm in the first place. Restorative justice gives our peacemaking some concrete tools and puts conflict transformation into practice.[1]

Holding the High Ground
Respect
Responsibility
Relationship
Repair

Like travelers in unfamiliar territory, it can be helpful to have a map to help us navigate interpersonal relationships. All of our tools and resources are more helpful when we are clear on how we want to live our lives and treat other people.

It's easy to assume that we live by certain high ground values more than we actually do. Our core beliefs and negative self-talk all too easily override our best intentions when we don't stay conscious. A commitment to live by specific values helps focus our attention and direct our behavior.

While high ground traits can be represented by a variety of different characteristics, the helpfulness comes from naming just a few that form a comprehensive whole: with just a few words we capture a wide range of adult behavior. In this example we'll come back to some of the core values of restorative justice and put them in a larger context.

Because keeping the high ground is an on-going process, self-awareness is needed. It's not about being perfect—no one is always on the high ground, but we can practice being there, staying there, and getting back there when we fall short.

Respect

Respect is the basic building block that makes peace possible. When respect is present, the ground is fertile and anything is possible. Can you imagine a healthy relationship that wasn't built on respect? How can there be trust without respect?

An easily overlooked aspect of respect is self-respect. Self-respect lays the foundation for respect for others and is a great litmus test for how well we are attending to the self-awareness and self-acceptance so essential to healing. For example, when we've done something hurtful in a relationship and drop into feelings of shame or defensiveness, or close down in some other way, we know we still have work to do.

Respect for ourselves and others is a strong indication that we are living into the truth of interbeing.

Responsibility

In restorative justice, responsibility as a value tends to focus on responsibility for the specific harm done. Without responsibility, there can be no real repair, especially of damaged relationships. In the broader context of a high ground map we go right to one of life's most important lessons: that as adults, we are 100% responsible for ourselves.

Thoughts may come unbidden, but what we do with those thoughts is our responsibility. Our feelings, emotions, needs and behaviors—we are responsible for all of it. A commitment to self-responsibility helps us avoid hooking our happiness to the thoughts and behaviors of others and avoid the associated disappointment. Self-responsibility keeps us in our power.

So much of our dissatisfaction comes from the expectations we place on others. We tend to want other people to think and behave in a certain way. If only they would do XYZ we'd be so happy! When they don't, we easily fall prey to resentments that build up over time and suck the life out of relationships.

If we make our unhappiness into a problem caused by someone else, we lose our power to change the situation. Instead, we can look more deeply at our own thoughts and behavior. We can gain insight into what we are really longing for and what we need to do. Satisfaction is not something given by someone else but comes from our own felt experience. Healthy relationships are not based on a 50/50 mentality but on each person taking 100% self-responsibility.

Yes, we will be triggered by other people, but how we respond is up to us. Yes, we have needs, but once we are adults, it is our responsibility to take care of ourselves and assure that our needs are met. It is not someone else's responsibility to read our minds and meet our needs.

By the same token, we are not responsible for anyone else's thoughts, feelings, needs, or emotions. We may play a role in triggering them, and we can take accountability for that, but how they respond is ultimately their responsibility.

Relationship

An emphasis on interpersonal relationships, here in the larger context of our interbeing, supports us in giving priority to relationships over our own individual interests. That can seem overly idealistic and unrealistic until we realize that so many of our most basic needs can only be met through healthy relationships. An example that often comes up for me is giving priority to a particular relationship over my desire to be "right" and get my way. Relationships teach us the beauty and value of communication and cooperation.

Giving priority to relationships is really only possible once we realize that our wellbeing is linked to the wellbeing of other people, other beings, and the Earth as a whole. When we put relationship first, we move beyond habitual patterns of egotism, self-defense, and apathy. Everything changes because nothing puts us on the spot like relationships!

Giving priority to relationships means we do our best to express our needs clearly and listen to the needs of others. It doesn't mean staying in relationships that are unhealthy. Sometimes the best way to honor a relationship is to make clear boundaries and keep a respectful distance. Sometimes, despite our best intentions, we need to leave certain relationships in order to take care of ourselves. But we don't have to blame, resent, or degrade other people in the process.

Self-responsibility and giving priority to relationships lays a foundation for respect and the ability to repair damaged relationships. It's also a two-way street and not a linear process since respect is the basic building block of relationship.

Repair

With respect and self-responsibility, and in the context of open and healthy relationships, it is possible to repair harm whenever it occurs. By *harm* I mean anything that was done or not done, said or not said, that caused stress and a break in the sense of connection. The need for repair is a natural aspect of healthy relationships—we do trigger each other sometimes!

A commitment to repair harm demonstrates our care and the lived reality of interbeing—with or without repairing the harm, we'll be feeling the consequences of whatever it was that happened. Even in the most loving relationships, our needs for safety and communication, for trust and understanding, (to name just a few) are deep! Without ongoing repair it is practically inevitable that relationships will run aground on the shores of resentment and disconnection.

We can talk about qualities such as honesty and integrity all we want without it amounting to much. Talk *is* cheap. But when we have some actual tools for transforming conflict—and the commitment to use them—then we can move beyond talk and put our best intentions into practice. Use these tools to help you be who you want to be, not as another excuse to beat yourself up when you fall short.

Any honest intention to stay on the high ground will include a commitment to ongoing personal healing, self-awareness, and self-care. Mindfulness, nature-based practices, and the full range of all our resources (outlined in the previous chapter) help us come back to center when we're knocked off balance and come back to the high ground.

Intimate Relationships

Sexuality has long been a target of the life-denying worldview with far reaching effects. When the life energy inherent in sex is disparaged and negated, it doesn't go away, it goes underground, and society becomes twisted into perversion and hypocrisy. Jerry Falwell, Jimmy Swaggart, and Ted Haggard are some names that come to my mind in the context of sexual hypocrisy.

A focus on sexuality reminds us that there are thousands of years of abuse to be healed.

Bringing mindfulness, honesty, and other mature qualities into sex, we move beyond the momentary pleasure of orgasm and into a deeper communion where heart-opening love and bliss are possible. A mindful approach to sexuality can be a powerful way to heal the abuse and shame from which so many suffer. Through conscious lovemaking we dissolve boundaries and help create a more peaceful world.[2]

Intimate relationships are the perfect place to practice seeing the divine in another. But the presence of spirit doesn't keep intimate relationships from being the most challenging of all. Our lovers call us out on things we try so hard to keep hidden. Added together, our warped preconceptions, poor role models, and psychic wounds create a shaky foundation for intimacy. It then becomes all too easy to question and give up on relationships when we hit the inevitable rough spots.

Many of us have been led to believe that intimate relationships are supposed to be easy. We just need to meet the right person and it's happily ever after. It's a convenient belief that fits with the immaturity, the fear of conflict, and the lack of training and tools so prevalent today. But if interpersonal relationships are the fertile ground where real maturity can be cultivated, then intimate relationships are the most fertile of all because so much is at stake and we are seen the most, well, nakedly.

When engaged in consciously, an intimate relationship is where we can do the deepest healing. When an atmosphere of safety and respect is created we can practice meeting the basic relationship needs that were not adequately met when we were young. Longings such as those for connection, trust, acceptance, and unconditional love are essential aspects of our humanity that are with us for life.

I notice with my partner that taking the time to figure out what creates a sense of safety, and what we can do to soothe each other when we are triggered, thaws out places long frozen. For me, this involves noticing the numbness that comes when I am triggered and the impulse to shut down. Once I'm aware of this, I can stay with my own experience and communicate what is happening to my partner.

Bringing consciousness and acceptance to the habitual response, and doing something that keeps us connected in those crucial moments, has deepened our relationship in profound ways. Instead of closing down, we open to our shared vulnerability and longing. When the invitation to be present can be answered with openness and heart-felt communication it changes everything.

I remember an experience that brought much of what has been discussed in this book together in the context of intimacy.

I was on an evening walk in my favorite local place—forested open space on the edge of town. It was a beautiful evening after prolonged rain, fresh and clear and crisp. I was taking my time, walking slower than usual, and really taking in the beauty of everything around me.

I saw a woman approaching from the opposite direction on the trail and I heard her softly singing; we made eye contact, said hello, and continued to move in the directions we were going. She continued to sing and I was happy my presence hadn't interrupted that.

A short distance up the trail I stopped to take in the trees, creek, and a particular bird. The woman approached and stood before me, saying that when we made eye contact she knew she wanted more connection. We introduced ourselves and smiled at each other.

In a very natural way it quickly came out that I lived nearby with my partner and that she too lived in the area and was single. She told me she had just returned from a silent meditation retreat and was feeling her heart break open and essence pouring in. I responded in the limited way that words seem to allow that I was so happy that she had included me and that her opening and openness brought me great joy.

We stood there, on this lovely evening, enfolded by an ash tree forest, much loved by bears and birds, with the creek gurgling in our ears, and looked at each other. I felt a strong sexual attraction, after all, she seemed to be presenting herself so openly and her presence was so radiant and beautiful. But beyond the lust, I felt *my* heart open, and I noticed that what I was really feeling in that moment was my own aliveness—connected and celebratory!

We walked up the trail together a short ways and she started to take a faint path up the hill, saying that she had never been that way and needed to ground herself. I thanked her for the connection and we wished each other well. I watched her move up the slope and then proceeded up the main trail, trying to take in what had just happened.

When I got to the bridge where I normally pause to remember the bears I had seen there, and to appreciate the view of the mountains before turning back and heading home, I lingered longer than usual. I felt intimately connected to myself, the land, and spirit—to the energy that quickens the heart and makes life possible (and worth living). I felt that sexual impulse with no shame and felt it integrate into my larger sense of being—being human, being animal, being Earth, being spirit.

Later, when I told my partner Samhitta about what had happened, I felt again how being able to tell her my truth, and hear her truth in response, breathes fresh life into our relationship. It opened the door to a soulful conversation about our needs and how we were feeling in relation to each other and to life. It's not that there was anything wrong, only that (seemingly) natural kind of withholding that happens so easily in the familiarity of intimate relationship. Our sharing that morning, sitting together on the outskirts of our local farmer's market, was mirrored by the nearby creek rushing by, swollen with spring runoff, purging the stagnant pools and refreshing the whole artery with new oxygen and energy. There were things that were said that were scary—hard to say and hard to hear—things that even undermined our closeness on the surface for a short time, but deeper down our roots were being watered and refreshed.

Honesty *is* the best aphrodisiac I know of. The tender heart longs to be shown and seen, our full humanness felt and honored—all without judgment and hypocrisy. Honesty allows us to keep it real, to keep it human, to stay in integrity and choice. The richness of intimate relationships never fails to amaze me.

With the work of restoring interpersonal relationships we put our egos on the line and stretch our boundaries. We can be grateful for having practices and tools that allow us to stay grounded as we express the life energy that lives in us and longs for expression. We can meet life's challenges with increasingly open hearts and celebrate that we are moving toward realizing our highest potential and fulfilling our deepest desires.

Restorative Practice
What's Alive? [3]

This is an exercise you can do with an intimate partner, a friend, or anyone you would like a deeper connection with. You will need forty minutes and some kind of stopwatch or timer.

Begin by taking some deep, mindful breaths. Set an intention to be fully present to yourself and the other person.

One of you will begin by taking ten minutes to answer the question, "What is alive in you right now?" In other words, "What do you notice in your body, your heart, or your mind?" "What do you feel down deep?" "What do you most want to share and say?" Whatever you notice, think of it as aliveness, as life energy coursing through you.

Keep it as real and grounded in the present moment as possible. Pauses are okay and it's fine to share mostly thoughts, but at some point during your sharing tell the other person what you are feeling in your body.

The listener will practice deep listening and not interrupt the speaker.

After the ten minutes is up, the person who was listening will take ten minutes to respond to the same question, "What is alive in you right now?" Don't spend time commenting on what the other person has said. Speak from your own experience of what is alive in you.

After the second person is complete, you will each do another round of ten minutes using the same question, "What is alive in you right now?"

When the time is up, notice how you feel and thank each other before transitioning into the next activity.

Photo credit: Stephen R. Jones

"*Compassion is not necessarily soft—it can also be fierce and unwavering....Selfless action is far more courageous and powerful than action in defense or promotion of the self. Life works through us and we become a force of nature...Care and love flow naturally, without hesitation.*"

Chapter Eleven

Restoring Our Relationship to the World

Love and compassion are necessities, not luxuries.
Without them humanity cannot survive.
—The Dalai Lama

Through restorative practices we expand the sense of self beyond the personal and develop an ever-widening sense of identity and participation with the world. With a more secure sense of who we are and why we are here, energy that would otherwise be spent endlessly trying to satisfy the ego becomes available for service to others.

True service comes from a place of fullness, not neediness. It is about giving back because we have something to give, not about receiving anything in return. True service is an outpouring offered in a natural way. When we reach out to serve, we just do it, without attachment to particular outcomes; it is our compassion in action.

The collective rite of passage we find ourselves in calls us to live from the truth of interbeing. Since this cuts against the grain of our habitual thinking and behavior, healing the relationship to self, nature, and other people is essential. These foundations allow our service to flow from a ground of health—from a place of clarity and resilience—and keep our good intentions from being undercut by the ego.

Here, too, there is reciprocity. We attend to our restoration in order to be of service to others and at the same time, serving others is a vehicle for our own restoration. Many research studies have found that people who regularly do volunteer work live longer, are less depressed, and have a greater sense of wellbeing.

The deeper benefits of service were brought home to me one night, at a talk by veterans on the emotional costs of war. A Vietnam vet spoke about the trauma he experienced and his post-war alcoholism and drug abuse. He told the crowd that what saved him was getting involved with a group dedicated to helping veterans. It was this service to others that got him out of his head and jump-started his recovery.

Embracing Openness, Compassion, and Love

When we allow ourselves to feel our own pain and be in our own vulnerability, we can be with others in an honest way. Essential qualities of the mature human being, such as openness, compassion, and love flow like a river from a deep, pure source.

There's not much talk about openness, compassion, and love in the life-denying society. Sure, these qualities come up on occasion, but they are not taken very seriously. With few wise elders and role models to teach us and little knowledge and experience of who we really are, the traits most associated with transformation lie dormant under the surface of our being.

Compassion is to feel or suffer *with* another. It is not about "fixing," but "being with" in a state of real presence. If we are focused on trying to fix people, we are not fully present to them and whatever they are experiencing. Wanting to fix and have things turn out a certain way blocks open-heartedness and flow, and turns service into a project or campaign, pulling us out of our hearts and into our heads.

Compassion is not necessarily soft—it can also be fierce and unwavering. When the heart leads the way, we are less inclined to weigh the pros and cons of what's in it for us. Selfless action is thus far more courageous and powerful than action in defense or promotion of the self. Life works through us and we become a force of nature. It is not about being nice or doing something because we think we "should." Care and love flow naturally, without hesitation.

It is amusing to me that I'm writing a book that, in the end, has so much to do with love. I recall a leadership training I was in many years ago. At the end of it, we were asked to write a brief note to ourselves about what we wanted to remember. The note was then going to be put it in a self-addressed envelope and sent to us six months later. The message I wrote read, simply, "Love is the answer." I remember feeling surprised and even a little embarrassed by what I had written. The workshop did not have anything to do with love and no one was coaching me on the topic. It seemed to come out of nowhere. Six months later, when I received the note in the mail, I still wasn't quite sure how to relate to its message but it made a little more sense—some kind of seed had been planted.

Many years later, after beginning the process of "doing my work" and setting out on the peacemaker path I was asked to do a similar exercise. This time I immediately knew what to write: "Ah, yes, love is *still* the answer." And now, later still, with more restorative practice under my belt, I celebrate having experienced first hand my essence as awareness itself and the openness, compassion, and love that flow from that source. I celebrate becoming conscious enough to experience what love really is. Love, not as a fleeting emotion, but as an expression of what I really am; flowing from beyond the personal and transforming all it touches.

Restorative Practice
Self Care

In these turbulent times it is important that we take care of ourselves physically, mentally, and spiritually. To this end, it can be helpful to inquire into our overall level of self-care.

This can be particularly important for people involved in intense forms of service work and activism, where there is such a strong tendency to engage in behaviors that are self-destructive such as drug and alcohol abuse, overwork, poor diet, and lack of exercise. These are often justified by emphasizing the difficult and/or time-consuming nature of the work.

The point of this exercise is not to be moralistic or dogmatic, but to simply bring attention to the issue of self-care and invite self-awareness and reflection.

Take some time to reflect on your overall level of self-care. Do you feel good about how you are living your life and treating your body?

Are you engaging in behaviors that you don't feel good about? If so, name the specific behaviors for yourself. Are these behaviors limiting your effectiveness or ability to sustain your energy? If so, in what ways are they limiting?

Are there any changes you want to make in your level of self-care? If so, decide on some concrete and doable steps you can take.

Revisit these questions periodically.

Activism as Restorative Practice

My activism pays the rent on being alive and being here on the planet. If I weren't active politically, I would feel as if I were sitting back eating at the banquet without washing the dishes or preparing the food.

—Alice Walker

We conclude our walk together on the path of active peace with activism. Because we aren't separate from other people, other species, and the planet, it is natural to feel compelled to act on behalf of life. Because we are not separate, life-affirming action is an important part of our individual and collective healing.

While the word "activism" can include a lot of baggage associated with anger and violence, and could be defined in a number of ways, it really just means taking action in the political arena. And politics, while that word too can easily be loaded down with lots of images and ideas, is simply the process of civic engagement. So activism is synonymous with active citizenship and it's pretty obvious that we need more of that these days.

Because it is interpersonal work that includes deeply personal aspects encompassing the territory of self-righteousness, frustration, grief, rage, and burnout, nothing puts our restorative practices to the test quite like activism. With so much devastation all around us we are constantly being challenged with endless opportunities for the mind and ego to get all worked up. When we do engage politically, the temptation is strong to do so with expectations that things will work out a certain way and that change will happen fast. We regularly face disappointment over both the quality and the pace of change.

It was only after fifteen years of doing my best as an activist without mindfulness and basic relationship skills that it finally started to dawn on me that we really are all in this together. I was in Nova Scotia organizing a coalition of environmental groups to lobby for habitat protection for the mainland moose population. I was doing my usual thing, with my usual assumptions about how "they," in this case, provincial land managers, would oppose "us."

At some point along the way, one of the environmental group leaders I was working with suggested that we invite provincial representatives to participate in the coalition. I was taken aback and I didn't agree to her request, but there was something in her desire for honest collaboration that touched me. She planted a seed that subtly changed the way I approached all of my interactions with government officials from that moment forward. Over time, that seed grew into a deep knowing that prioritizing relationships is the way forward.

That interaction helped me begin to put my activism in a larger context and start to see the limits of the "us versus them" approach. Stepping all the way back to put activism in the context of creating a nonviolent world, where it is clear that virtually everything about society needs to change, allowed me to see that a more peaceful and relational approach was basic common sense.

Connecting with our own life force energy and the longings that manifest through that energy, gives us the clean burning fuel we need as activists. It is not anger and outrage that we need. What we need is the ability to be in touch with all our emotions as they arise—all the anger, sadness, grief, and fear—and the longing for life that lies underneath. Without this kind of presence we easily get trapped into feeling like victims and lose touch with the felt sense of interrelatedness and the clarity that comes with it.

We are called to challenging and simultaneous tasks. The first is to build the foundations of a life-affirming society. The second is to bear witness and respond to the destruction and suffering that surrounds us. This is why we need mindfulness and nature-based practices, and interpersonal skills and practice more than ever.

Restorative Practice
Gratitude

As we face the pain and suffering in the world, it is easy to get caught up in selective vision, focusing primarily on what is wrong, damaging, and ugly. Such a limited view can drive us into a deep pit of despair.

Practicing gratitude is an elegant remedy for bringing more of reality into focus. Appreciating what we have puts things into perspective. When gratitude becomes a way of life we become more resilient and whatever life throws at us becomes more workable.

Spend some time practicing gratitude every day for the next week. This can include gratitude for who you are, what you do, what you have; for your friends and family, and for your health. It can encompass gratitude for the beauty and wonder in the world, for other species, and for life itself. There is no limit to the gratitude that can be expressed.

First thing in the morning before getting out of bed, and last thing before falling asleep are potent times to feel and express your gratitude.

> *Notice any shift in your consciousness that practicing gratitude brings. Notice if it helps you feel more alive and interconnected.*
>
> *After the week is over, decide if you will continue with this practice and, if you do, what your practice will look like.*

Mourning, Support, and Real Empowerment

While psychology seeks to liberate people on the personal level, it continues to mostly fail at putting that healing in social, environmental, and political context. It is increasingly urgent that the human psyche not be treated as an isolated entity, like a fish outside of the water that sustains it.

The pain we feel for other people, other species, and the world as a whole, is normal and healthy. It is feedback that tells us everything is connected and that so much is out of balance. When that pain is blocked, so too is a vital part of our humanness. Tapping into the root of our despair and pain we find the sincerest of longings right there in our life energy.

Stepping back from all our thoughts about right and wrong, good and bad, and just being with the pure longing, opens our hearts to what is truly precious. In this heart-centered place of connection our thoughts and actions naturally become more restorative. Staying with our natural vulnerability, we shift from the habitual protective responses such as anger, self-righteousness, and blame, without any effort whatsoever. Life longs for life, not punishment and revenge.

We are in the territory here of real empowerment and the key that unlocks that door is the pain itself and the mourning we bring to it.[1] Pain is an invitation to feel and mourn. When we accept this invitation we align with our hearts, our life energy, and life itself. We are in the flow, with no separation.

True mourning opens us and honors our fullness. It keeps it real by bringing consciousness to what we are really feeling and wanting. We attend to our inner experience when it really has our full attention, when we are vulnerable and open-hearted.

True mourning is a practice. It doesn't argue with what is. And it isn't resignation either. Like gratitude, true mourning aligns us with life. When we mourn, we come more fully alive, and that is the most powerful transformational force there is. The deeper the sorrow, the greater the joy.

Action arising out of a process of mourning will have clarity and integrity, a resonance with life. It won't necessarily look a certain way—there is still room for the full range of expression and emotion—but it will have an attunement to the heart and be more conscious.

The honest expression of anger, grief, despair, and pain is not the norm in our culture. Mourning as a regular practice is almost unheard of. Asking for help is not encouraged either. But if we are to move through life feeling truly empowered, mourning with the support of other people may very well be essential.

So here's another restorative practice: Find your tribe, the people you can trust with your life. They are out there. Ask for support, accept it as graciously as you can, and offer your support in return when its needed. When you ask for support you give a gift to others. Through their support of you, they know they matter. It's another way to live into the truth of interbeing. We aren't meant to do it alone.

I have benefited so much from being a part of a men's circle and various learning groups. Despite feeling like a fairly well resourced person at this point in my life, I have felt the power of being witnessed and blessed by others. There really is no substitute for it as far as I can tell. We *really* aren't meant to do it alone.

Opening to support required me to make a big stretch in the direction of self-care and trust. I have vivid memories of how challenging it was to ask for support for a particular training I wanted to do—a "street retreat" led by Fleet Maull.[2] We would travel to Denver with no money and only the clothes on our backs and one blanket each. We would live on the streets for three days and nights, eat at soup kitchens, and sleep on sidewalks or in parks.

In the tradition of Buddhist monks begging for their food, we would also beg for the money needed to get us home on the bus on the fourth day.

The whole thing was a challenge, a deep plunge into "not knowing." Begging the bus fare (asking for support from strangers) was one of the most challenging aspects of the experience, but it wasn't the hardest part.

The hardest part was built into the process well ahead of leaving for Denver. Again, in the spirit of the Buddhist begging practice, we were required to ask friends and family to contribute the money for the course's tuition. Writing those letters asking for support was more intimidating to me than the prospect of living on the streets of Denver for three days and nights and begging bus fare from strangers. I also experienced the discomfort that can come when support *is* offered—how thoughts of unworthiness can kick in and make it hard to graciously accept support.

A more recent experience brought home the potency of allowing the humbling Earth to hold my grief and need for support. I was co-guiding a wilderness rite of passage trip where the students would be doing a three-day solo fast. (Throughout our existence, we humans have gone into the wilderness to purify ourselves, seek a vision, solidify a sense of purpose, and/or mark a passage into a new stage of life). On the evening before their last full day and night in camp, we participate together in a grief ritual. Understanding how unspoken and unintegrated grief blocks and limits our energy, we open the space where grief can be fully and safely expressed and transmuted into life force. (The students are then more able to move beyond old patterns and hone clear intentions for new directions and identities when they are on their solos.)

Held by the land and the community of people, by the aspens and the creek just below the wailing station, we can intimately feel how the Earth invites our animal bodies to open to the honesty of our pain and deepest longings. People move forward one at a time while the rest of us chant and shake our rattles hard. Once in position, the person grieving can raise an arm if she or he would like support from one or more people.

The last time I did this ritual, when I was ready to take my turn I knew that nothing much was going to happen without the support of at least one person. I knelt above the creek and immediately signaled my desire for support. Once I felt myself held tight by another human the tears began to flow and the words and release came.

Some students may be surprised by how willingly and enthusiastically their guides participate in this ritual right along side of them. But we know how important the opportunity is, how rare, and how our wilderness setting offers the perfect place for it. Our tears move us out of consensus reality and into the flow—making space for dark waters and ancestors, nighthawks and night walks, oil-soaked seabirds and fish-netted dolphins, macheteed Rwandans and Syrian refugees.

I think of grief as the raw emotion, mourning as the practice of being with that emotion. Both provide the fertile ground where compassion grows. Both move us out of habitual patterns— numbness and apathy—and open the heart to interbeing and love.

Both mourning and asking for support can be mindfulness practices. We can notice the resistance and everything that happens internally in response. Both keep us in our vulnerability, where the energy of our longing resides. In that honesty is the empowerment to come together and co-create the world we want.

The Integrative Function of Activism

Well over 2,000 years ago Aristotle observed that we are political animals. Political action expresses important aspects of who we are and, from Aristotle on, astute observers have linked activism to psychological health and maturity. The pioneering psychologist Abraham Maslow found that:

> Self-actualizing people are, without one single exception, involved in a cause outside their own skin, in something outside of themselves. They are devoted, working at something....which fate has called them to somehow and which they work at and which they love, so that the work-joy dichotomy in them disappears.[3]

Modern researchers are doing their part to prove and quantify the benefits of activism. They use words such as *wellbeing, vitality,* and *flourishing* to describe the greater sense of aliveness they see and measure in activists.[4] While individual acts of activism are empowering in themselves, what is more important are the qualities and characteristics, such as confidence and compassion, that lead to activism in the first place.

Activists such as Joanna Macy, Andrew Harvey, and Vandana Shiva exemplify the aliveness that comes with giving back to the world in a conscious way. I have had the honor of being in the presence of these people and they are forces of nature, powerful and magnetic. Their lives are testimony to the healing benefits of activism, to the integration and synergy that is created when people move from the deep truth of interbeing.

Because of interbeing, true healing doesn't happen in isolated bubbles, but in the context of the world and the relationships that surround and penetrate us like the air we breathe. Activism pushes us to see the big picture and know as felt sense and lived experience that everything is connected. We come alive to ourselves and everything that supports life.

The Shadow Side of Activism

Activists are, however, not somehow magically exempt from the unconsciousness that is the norm in our society. Many activists are motivated by psychic wounds of various sorts and use their activism, however unconsciously, as a way to heal and empower themselves. In the shadow of many activists we once again find the belief in separateness, this time pestering those who talk the most about the interconnectedness of everything.

I recall my own sense of feeling like a victim, my unprocessed grief, my self-righteousness, and my failure to see things on the systems level. I was quick to judge and condemn what I perceived as apathy in other people but spent no time reflecting on their lives or really listening to them. The unconscious aspects of ourselves form our shadows and I cast as big a one as anybody and carried it into my work as an activist.

A lack of self-awareness limits the ability to appreciate the psychological experience of others. I see this playing out on a regular basis in the strategies and tactics activists commonly use—the creation of enemy images, and using blame, shame, and fear to bring about change. If these were effective approaches it would be one thing, but they aren't.

In reflecting on my own experience, I've come to believe that the tactics of blame, shame, and fear do not contribute to success. Any victories I was involved in—stopping multi-million dollar hazardous waste incinerators from being built in Florida and North Carolina, stopping a cement kiln in Georgia from burning hazardous waste—could have been achieved without making anybody into an enemy and creating more violence in the world (and I'll elaborate on this soon).

Beyond what felt like successes were many more instances of not getting what I wanted, and getting trapped in resentment and animosity as a result. When I look back on how consistently I relied on shame and blame in my lobbying, I shake my head in disbelief, but at least I don't have to wonder anymore why nobody wanted to talk to me.

The tactics of blame, shame, and fear may have helped bring about positive changes in the past, but let's consider the context and scope of those changes. However significant they might seem, they did not avert the disaster toward which we are heading. Racism, sexism, militarism, war, poverty, and climate change all continue to run rampant. The task before us is greater than any we have faced before. More than ever, we are called to use means that are consistent with the ends we wish to achieve.

Many activists hang on tight to anger and outrage, believing this to be the fuel that motivates them and keeps them going. This is unfortunate, partly because it's just not true, and partly because when the mind is overtaken by anger, stress is the unavoidable result. When under stress, the attributes we most need for restoring ourselves and society become smothered by fear and self-righteousness.

While anger is a natural response that can help us cut through nonsense and get to the point, when we look deeply we find the aquifer sustaining our activism is not anger but love. When our anger, grief, and pain can be recognized as coming from the wellspring of love and care for the world, and when the pain can be grieved and the love honored, everything changes. The energy of strong emotions are transformed into awareness, fierce compassion, and action grounded in the open heart and the truth of interbeing.

At the core of environmental success stories is the deep love and care that people have for their families and communities, for the beautiful land that enfolds and nurtures them, and the other species they share that land with, other beings who bring joy and fullness to life.

The last thing the world needs at this pivotal moment is for our love to be overshadowed by anger.

Scott leads a peacemaking teach-in at Freedom Plaza inWashington D.C. during Occupy in 2011

"Whatever your style of activism and the situations you find yourself in—every moment presents opportunities for awareness and connection to your deepest self, to your heart and your care and your love. That connection is the source of peace and transformation."

Chapter Twelve

Restorative Activism

Do whatever you must with people, but never shut anyone out of your heart, even for a moment.

—Neem Karoli Baba

We move now from talking about activism in a general way, to activism that prioritizes relationships and consistent nonviolence. I call it *restorative activism* because it heals the activist at the same time it contributes to healing society and the Earth. In terms of the personal benefits, this form of activism is a constant reminder to see others and ourselves with conscious awareness. We take care of ourselves and avoid feeding destructive emotions and unhealthy levels of stress. We cut ourselves the slack we need and embrace the practices that support us.

In terms of the collective benefit, restorative activism limits our unconscious lashing out and contributing more resentment, shame, and other forms of violence to the world. As any parent or mentor knows, people learn more from what we do than what we say. Sowing the seeds of life-affirming beliefs and values through our actions is much more powerful than going around telling people what they should do. Through consistent nonviolence we put interbeing into action.

Mindfulness, nature-based practices, relationship skills, and an expanded sense of self all combine to support a transpersonal approach to activism. Transpersonal awareness moves us out of the ego and all the attachments that come with it—to be in control, to be right, to be important, to be liked. When we see the bigger picture of reality, we can take ourselves less seriously and give priority to relationships, even the most challenging.

From this place of transpersonal awareness we can stay grounded, even in the face of the ignorance, chaos, and uncertainty that could otherwise overwhelm us. Despite how dire things may seem, we train ourselves for a marathon and not a sprint (remember, there is no quick fix). Awareness, openness, compassion, and love are the basis of a sacred approach to activism that goes to the roots of the crisis we face.

Restorative activism begs the question: What would be possible if every activist had real training and capacity as a peacemaker?

Three Capacities

When engaged in an ongoing way, active peace builds capacities we may never have even known we had. As I've thought about the capacities most needed for the work of social change, I always come back to the *Three Tenets* of the Zen Peacemaker Order founded by Bernie Glassman: not knowing, bearing witness, and compassionate action. I believe these capacities will stand the test of time as qualities worth cultivating in the shift to a nonviolent world.

Not Knowing

> *In the beginner's mind there are many possibilities, in the expert's, there are very few.*
> —Shunryu Suzuki

We spend a lot of time and energy trying to be secure, trying to control the present and predict the future. We invest heavily in hopes and pleasant outcomes. We find comfort and security in our ideas of right and wrong, good and bad. We want the world to be a certain way. We want to know! But one of the few things we *can* be certain about is how uncertain life is.

The trait or capacity of not knowing is a way to face the groundless nature of reality. It's not that we all of a sudden go stupid and literally don't know anything. Instead, it's an acknowledgement that impermanence is the name of the game—that there is no final security or certainty. Not knowing has an open quality.

When we think we know, we have at least one foot in the past, as we rely on past experience and learning. We all do this of course—it is basic to our survival and development. The restorative task is to see how this kind of thinking limits us.

The implications of embracing not knowing are boundless. In my own life, not knowing helps me go beyond "us-versus-them" thinking and see even those I am most challenged by as fellow travelers. My suffering lessens as I loosen my grip on what I think is "right" and how things "should" be. I feel more and more relaxed as I stop acting like I have, or should have, all the answers. This frees up energy and I find myself more present, open, curious, and creative.

Surrendering to the truth of not knowing is a big step, especially for activists. Because the pull is so strong to think it is our job as activists to know—to know what is right, what justice demands, what the world needs, etc.—there is no more challenging arena for the practice of not knowing than activism.

Not knowing doesn't mean giving up our hopes and visions for a better world. The energy of our longing is sacred and powerful. But loosening our attachments to specific outcomes keeps us flexible. We can relax into not knowing and still do our work. We can still advocate for "our" truth with intelligence and persistence. We can still hold people accountable for the harm they cause. In fact, the likelihood of real accountability increases dramatically when we meet other people on equal ground, where nothing is certain and everything is possible.

Bearing Witness

> *Knowing that nothing need be done is the place from which we begin to move.*
>
> —Gary Snyder

We are all confronted by a lot these days—disturbing news and images, the suffering of people and other species, our own fear and anxiety. Mindfulness and not knowing build the capacity to see, and be honest about, what is happening around us and work with our reactions. This increases our ability to move through pain and uncertainty with real presence and resilience.

Not knowing, not needing to have all the answers, means we don't need to act immediately to fix things, but can instead *bear witness*. Bearing witness is an active, nonjudgmental awareness of what is happening. It is seeing, feeling, and experiencing what is actually there—the raw data—unencumbered by our stories about what is happening.

I've noticed how not adding "my stuff" requires ongoing self-awareness. Having a kind of soft focus on my internal experience, even while most of my attention is directed outward, helps keep me from adding my projections onto other people and situations. I'm learning to make a practice out of noticing my own triggering and judgments, my feelings and emotions, even as I pay attention to what is happening around me. As imperfect as I am at this, it is nonetheless allowing me to see more clearly and be more present.

A commitment to truth and restorative practice leads us to a place where we can see the world with less filtering and numbness. Our perception is heightened and the likelihood of responding with intelligence, when and if we do respond, is greatly enhanced. Bearing witness helps us meet each situation and experience in a fresh and honest way.

We will still fall into unconscious, reactive modes. We will still get triggered and angry, still drop into blame, resentment, and judgment. But we are building capacities that help us to work with whatever comes up. Throughout it all we can connect with the love and compassion that brings us to care for other beings and the world in the first place.

Compassionate Action

> *Compassion is not the same as doing good, or being nice.*
> *Compassion functions freely, with no hesitation, no lim-*
> *itation. It happens with no effort, the way you grow hair,*
> *the way your heart beats....It does not take any conscious*
> *effort. Someone falls, you pick them up.*
>
> —John Daido Loori

Not knowing and bearing witness lay the groundwork for compassionate action by accessing our innate wisdom, basic goodness, and love. Seeing people and situations more clearly, we naturally respond from a place of connection.

Compassionate action does not mean weak or wishy-washy action. The ingredients that give rise to compassion also give rise to courage and represent real maturity. Through exploring our inner terrain we become secure enough to be vulnerable, and owning our vulnerability integrates and frees our energy. We don't have to hide our love anymore.

Connected to our deepest longings, we can be present to insecurity without being swept away by it. We can be present to fear without becoming it.

From the more integrated center of gravity we have cultivated, a fierce love rises. The lover and warrior bow to each other gracefully, while the kings and queens of the psyche dance with the magicians and fools. We've increased our bandwidth, become less dogmatic, and move with more multi-layered ease.

As peacemakers and restorative activists, it's no longer all about getting our way or feeling better. Without even knowing it, we train ourselves to be more present and trustworthy. Without any effort, we act with less calculation of costs and benefits, and compassionate action flows naturally. And since everything is constantly changing, the next situation will be different, and the opportunity will be there to return to not knowing and bearing witness.

I remember a Greenpeace protest where I was locked with another protester in a steel box that we used to block a railroad track spur leading to a chemical company. The company was considering starting to manufacture chlorofluorocarbons (CFCs), the compounds linked to destruction of the ozone layer, and we wanted to send a strong message that this was dangerous for the planet and a bad business decision.

The box was about eight feet long, five feet wide, and five feet tall. We had provisions to last us several days. We had air holes, which also served as small windows, and a battery for lights and small fans. We had radios for communicating with colleagues and the media. We were prepared to stay for as long as it took to convince the company to not go into the CFC business.

The space was small but there was plenty of room to practice not knowing, bearing witness, and compassionate action—if I'd only had the ability at the time.

There was nearly complete uncertainty about how law enforcement would respond. Would our colleagues, there to help keep us safe and alert the media, be arrested and taken away? Would the fan give out and the heat inside the box become oppressive? How would I get along with my colleague in such close quarters? Would one of us freak out? How long would we be in the box? What would happen when we came out? There was absolutely no way to know what would happen from one minute to the next.

With conscious awareness of not knowing, I would have been able to be much more relaxed and open throughout the process.

In terms of bearing witness, there was a lot that I could have paid attention to in a conscious, self-connected way. I could have been present to my own experience of each moment and the shifting interpersonal dynamics between me and my partner. When the sheriff deputies started pounding away on the top of box with sledgehammers trying to open the lid, there was deafening noise (fortunately we had hearing protection) that demanded attention, along with the danger associated with the heavy steel lid of the box, which was large and would be hard to avoid if it fell in on us. My companion, afraid she was about to be seriously hurt, started having a panic attack. And all the while, I was doing media interviews over two-way radio where I tried to leverage the chaos and focus on why we were there in the first place. In a way, I was doing my best to ignore all the things I now believe are so worthy of attention.

And compassionate action? Of course it was there to some extent. Both of us were in the box, ultimately, because of our love and care for the world. It's just that, speaking for myself, I wasn't aware that this was why I was there; I thought I was mostly just pissed off at what was happening to the Earth. I wasn't particularly heart-connected under the best of circumstances, and I don't recall much heart-connection in that box that day. What I remember is a whole lot of stress and a sense of desperation.

The story ends with the deputies taking the "jaws of life" to the top of the box, making some cuts in the steel and going back to trying to pound in an opening with sledgehammers. The situation continued to feel dangerous and my partner continued to panic. We eventually told them we'd come out voluntarily and we did. We were promptly arrested and released without incident. We later heard that the company we were blockading decided to not manufacture CFC's.

Whatever your style of activism and the situations you find yourself in—it's really no different. Every moment presents opportunities for awareness and connection to your deepest self, to your heart and your care and your love. That connection is the source of peace and transformation.

We think we know, but we don't. We think we know how things are going to go today because they went a certain way yesterday and the day before. But there is no certainty in any of it. We can unconsciously move through our activities and our days, or we can bear witness to our own lives and the lives around us. And when it is time to act, we can do it from the heart, with love.

Restorative Practice
Bearing Witness

Here is an exercise that will give you a felt sense of how the practices outlined in this book can transform your activism. This exercise can be done alone or with a partner. In either case, you will feel the shift that is possible in how you view and approach the issues of the day.

Take whatever time you need to settle into your space and body.

When you feel settled and grounded, let an image arise of some social or environmental injustice. It could be an image of war, poverty, racism, or sexism. It may be an image of an environmental issue such as the Fukushima nuclear meltdown, a clearcut forest, an oil spill, or a factory farm. Take your time and let the image arise without forcing anything to happen.

There may be a whole scenario, a whole history that unwinds. Out of that, let your awareness find a single image that stands out.

Once you find a particular image, stay with it and notice the thoughts and emotions that arise. Notice anger, grief, and any sense of injustice. Let yourself have these thoughts and emotions without any pushing away or censorship.

Next, begin to let go of each thought that arises and focus your awareness on the actual feelings in your body. Stay with the original image and the sensations you notice.

Make space for any discomfort; allow whatever arises to be there. There is truth and a pure energy in whatever you are feeling.

Continue to notice when thoughts arise and let them go. Don't go into a story about good/bad, right/wrong. Stay with the feelings in your body.

Ask yourself, "What is the deep longing at the root of these feelings?" Take your time and let the longing surface. It might be a longing for security, safety, health, peace, or ease.

Feel the energy of this longing in your body. Notice the aliveness it brings when you simply allow it to be. Feel this energy as an essential part of your wholeness.

Stay with the life energy of the longing and bring the original image back into your awareness. Hold them both in your heart.

When you feel ready, let the image fade away and notice what you are left feeling. Imagine yourself acting in the world from this place, this level of awareness and attunement to your body. Would your action—your thoughts, words, and deeds—include more presence and compassion? How would that feel?

Spend some time reflecting on whatever this exercise leaves you with.

Restorative Justice Unleashed

Imagine if all the energy that goes into fighting other people and reinforcing the belief in separateness was instead directed at showing respect for people and giving priority to relationships. What if the five Rs of restorative justice—respect, relationship, responsibility, repair, and reintegration—were guiding principles of our activism? What if elected officials and other decision-makers adopted the five Rs and we could actually meet in an open field of trust and real dialogue?

Naive? Maybe, but is it less naive to think we can continue with business as usual and survive?

Restorative justice is a proven success—a grand success—and it's time to bring its principles and practices to bear on the full range of social and environmental issues and conflicts. When we transform the way we *approach* difficult issues, we greatly increase the odds of transformative outcomes. When life-affirming values are put into practice in the service of bringing out the best in people and tapping the collective wisdom, with that shift alone we've created a new and very different way of doing business. It's a way of doing business that, instead of entrenching separateness and division, actually facilitates the relationship building that allows the truth of interbeing to be experienced. In an atmosphere of safety and respect, when the defenses drop, what's left is the truth of who and what we really are. In an atmosphere of safety and respect, anything is possible!

As we saw in Chapter Ten, each of the five Rs of restorative justice sets a certain intention and specific questions flow from each one; taken together they lay out a framework for addressing harm. In the broad social context we're exploring in this section, the harm can also be potential harm; the principles and practices of restorative justice can be used to evaluate the potential consequences of specific actions and decisions.

In order to more fully explore how a restorative process could be used to address issues outside of the criminal justice system, we'll consider the example of British Petroleum's Deepwater Horizon oil spill in the Gulf of Mexico.

In choosing such an extreme event, an event that killed eleven workers and a tremendous amount of marine life, and caused such a huge amount of ecological and economic damage, my intention is to show the flexibility and potential of the process. I invite you to compare it, as imperfect, slow, and messy as it would likely be if used to address something as significant and complicated as the BP oil spill, with the bureaucratic, lawsuit driven process actually used to address the spill. You'll need to use your imagination and your common sense.

It's been several years since the explosion and the beginning of the spill on April 20, 2010. Has the harm to people and the environment been repaired? Has full responsibility been taken? Has systems-level change been made to assure that such a disaster will never—can never—happen again? I suspect the answer to all these questions is a resounding "No."

Obviously, there is no quick fix to something as disastrous as the BP oil spill, and I hope it will be equally obvious that what follows is not intended as such. I simply hold it up as a possibility—one that could serve to move us in a life-affirming, nonviolent direction.

It's important to remember that the context for the questions is an atmosphere of respect. Without respect nothing approaching full restoration is possible. In using this process in a situation where the harm has yet to occur, *respect* is the absolute starting point since people won't come to the table without it. When the harm has already occurred, as in a criminal justice context or with the BP oil spill, *responsibility* is the logical starting point since people won't come to the table, and there won't be respect, if responsibility hasn't been taken.

Remember too, that it's not your job or mine to answer these questions in isolation. Instead, with the understanding that this process is non-adversarial by nature, imagine a group of people who are most affected, and representatives of the groups most affected, coming together with those willing to take their share of responsibility (regulators, elected officials, and industry representatives). Add in some respected community members with no axe to grind—people who can see the big picture, and some facilitators responsible for orchestrating the process.

The many people in the sectors impacted—the families of those killed and injured, the oil and gas workers as a group, shrimpers, fisherman, property owners, the tourism industry, and environmentalists speaking on behalf of wildlife and the ecosystem—have already come together. They've elected the people who will represent their interests in the larger group and come to some initial shared understanding about the harm and who is responsible for it. How to repair the harm will come later, once the harm is fully understood and those responsible have had the opportunity to step forward. These stakeholder groups have already adopted and practiced the restorative mindset; they want healing, not revenge. The community representatives have taken lots of community input and are prepared to bring that pain and the local knowledge to the process.

Mechanisms are in place so the many people who can't be in the room and the public at large can have meaningful input. All meetings will be recorded, anyone who wants to will be able to see and hear every second of it.

Imagine the participants—the primary stakeholders—all sitting in a large circle where every voice counts, where everyone is respected. No table separates them. In the middle of the circle, each participant has placed something that reminds them why they are participating, a photograph perhaps. Imagine an opening statement acknowledging the pain and anger in the room and the enormity of the task ahead—the repair of a tremendous, nearly inconceivable amount of harm. Imagine a final reminder of the ground rules that will keep the process respectful and allow everyone to be heard, and a final reminder that this is a *healing circle*. Imagine everyone being invited to take some deep breaths and to connect with their highest selves in whatever way works for each. Then the questions unfold, in an order that makes sense, guided by the facilitators and with no artificial time constraints, with the ultimate intention of not punishment but repair of the harm.

Responsibility – What happened? What is the harm that resulted? How has the human community been harmed (e.g., physical/health, economic, social, cultural)? Which individuals have been harmed and how? How has the environment, other species, and the ecosystem as a whole been harmed? What are the ripple effects of the harm?

Who is responsible? Who will decide who is responsible? Who is voluntarily stepping up to take their share of responsibility?

Why did this happen/What is the context? What were the people who caused the harm thinking? What were the needs underlying the behaviors that led to the incident?

What are the contributing factors at the systems level?

How do the people responsible feel about their actions now? What is needed to encourage more self-responsibility?

Respect – Is respect being shown to everyone involved? Are the people who caused the harm being seen as full human beings better than their worst mistakes? Are those involved showing self-respect?

What does respect look like in this situation? What limits respect? What support is needed to encourage more respect?

Relationship – How have interpersonal, economic, and social relationships been damaged? Why are these relationships important?

Who needs to be involved as support for those harmed and those responsible for the harm so that everyone can participate fully?

Repair – What does repair of the harm (personal, interpersonal, economic, social, environmental, ecological, non-human beings) entail in this situation? Who will decide what constitutes full repair? Can there be a consensus?

What has already been done to repair the harm? Do those harmed feel restored?

Have the ripple effects of the harm been addressed and repaired? Have the relationships been restored? Has repair occurred on the community scale? Do the people who caused the harm feel restored?

Have steps been taken to ensure that an accident like this will not happen again? What systems-level changes have been made?

Is there more that needs to be done to repair the harm and, if so, what are some specific actions that can be taken? How can a process of restoration and repair be sustained over time (in this case, a very long time)? What structures need to be in place? Who will facilitate what?

What additional support (economic, material, psychological, spiritual, social/cultural) is needed to repair the harm when so much has been changed and getting back to "normal" isn't possible?

Can there be a consensus on an action plan? If there is no consensus on how to repair the harm, what are the options for moving forward?

Reintegration – Once the process of restoration and repair is completed (if that's possible), are those harmed willing to allow those who caused the harm to reintegrate back into society in a good way, without resentment or shame? To the extent that the answer is "no," the harm has not been fully repaired. What additional repair and support is needed to get beyond resentment?

Are those who caused the harm, assuming they have repaired the harm, willing and able to reintegrate back into society without feeling shame and resentment? To the extent that the answer is "no," the harm may not be fully repaired. What is needed to get to "yes"?

These questions, so basic and yet so big, outline a way to repair harm that is much more humane, holistic, and healing than business as usual. Many more questions would obviously follow those listed and much detail has been left out. But it *is* clear to me that this process is big enough, and compassionate enough, to hold the whole world in the circle of its care. It's big enough to hold the uncertainty and the challenges—the knowing that there are no easy answers or guarantees of a wonderful outcome that makes everyone happy.

Uncertainty about causes and impacts, and disagreements over how to best repair the harm, will not magically disappear. There will still be tendencies toward shame, blame, resentment, dishonesty, and lack of self-responsibility; but unlike current litigation-based mechanisms, these won't be the very foundation of the process.

The basic point is this: When people come together with a heart-felt intention to repair the harm, and demonstrate good faith in the process, trust can be built and the collective wisdom gathered.

A basic premise of restorative justice is that everyone participating does so voluntarily. A process focused on repairing the harm in the best way possible will be much more likely to gain the trust of those responsible for the harm than processes based on assessing blame and punishment.

My purpose in this section is to stimulate thought in the direction of conflict transformation and what really serves life. Hence, another guiding question can be: What is the life-serving and nonviolent response in this situation?

If we are serious about creating a nonviolent world, restorative values such as relationship and respect will have to find their place, not only in our hearts, but in our systems as well. Maybe we aren't there yet, but how hard are we trying?

On August 10, 2015 I sent an open letter to the Governor of Colorado, John Hickenlooper, asking him to establish a restor- ative process to address a recent spill of mining waste into the

Animas River upstream of Durango. Images had circulated of
this beautiful trout stream being turned orange by the pollution. I was developing my ideas for how to use the principles
and practice of restorative justice to address environmental and
other issues, and since Colorado is a stronghold of restorative
justice, I decided to write the letter and do some outreach.[1]

I didn't know anyone in Durango I could reach out to. I contacted
a local environmental group there and received no response.
I reached out to the leader of a stakeholder group organized
around mining waste issues in the region and he expressed a
little bit of curiosity but not much. I gave a copy of my letter
to the Governor to a neighbor who was a high-ranking Environmental Protection Agency official but heard nothing back.
I never received any response from the Governor's office. Some
of my restorative justice colleagues did respond, saying that
they would gladly volunteer to facilitate a restorative process.
I suppose it's safe to say that nothing much came out of that
particular effort, but it felt like a start.

I truly believe that a process like the one outlined above will
gain traction somewhere, sometime, and that once it does, the
momentum will build. I believe that virtually any social/political
issue where there is identifiable harm could be addressed using
these methods. That would include immigration, gun control
and gun violence, abuses of power, and the big issues of war and
peace. There really is no limit to the ways in which restorative
justice can transform our societies.

But let's do be honest that this approach, which transforms
activism into peacemaking, is a radical departure from business as usual. I know that when I started to give priority to
respect and relationships it changed everything about the way
I practice activism!

One of the main beauties of moving in a more restorative direction
is the inclusion of the big picture and the need for systems-level
change. For example, it would be hard to ever argue that the harm

caused by the BP oil spill disaster in the Gulf of Mexico was repaired as long as there was a strong likelihood that something similar will happen again. More than anything, victims often want to know that what happened to them—or their environment—will not ever happen again. And while getting to absolute certainty is usually not possible, in a restorative process a good faith effort will need to be made, otherwise it simply isn't restorative.

Maybe you'll bring the practice and principles of restorative justice to bear on a conflict near you. If you do, you'll have justice and life itself on your side. Just as Dr. King pointed out that, "The arc of the moral universe is long, but it bends toward justice." The arc of the universe itself is long, but it bends toward life.

Consistent Nonviolence

Be kind, for everyone you meet is fighting a great battle.
—Philo of Alexandria

The word "nonviolence" continues to be a powerful mantra in activist circles, but it has lost its deeper meaning. It seems that most any behavior short of obvious physical violence or property damage is readily deemed nonviolent. I have a somewhat different take.

When I hear angry diatribes or the all too familiar chant of "shame on you," it doesn't feel nonviolent. There is an energy there that aims to hurt and punish. I feel it in my body as stress and a shutting down of life energy. I also feel sadness and the frustration that comes with the sense that the big picture is not being seen—that the truth of interbeing has been lost.

When I spent time with Occupy activists in New York City and Washington, D.C., they were, for the most part and by some standards, nonviolent. But it was obvious enough that while they wanted to defeat injustice, many also wanted to punish and shame some people in the process. While many seemed to have chosen love (or wanted to), many were also hanging on to hate.

This created a toxic cloud that floated over an otherwise beautiful gathering. I spoke with many people there who longed for a more peaceful approach.

Action based on shame, blame, and "us-versus-them" thinking, is not only ineffective in bringing about the deep social transformation needed, it is counterproductive. It is one of the most common ways activists who understand interrelatedness on an intellectual level fail to put that understanding into practice. Many of us praise the pioneering work of Gandhi and Martin Luther King, Jr., but quickly abandon a principled stance on nonviolence when we don't get our way.

One of Martin Luther King, Jr.'s most profound principles of nonviolence is that nonviolence seeks to defeat injustice, not people. To do that requires choosing love over hate and realizing that there aren't "bad people" to blame. It just isn't that simple. What about the importance of worldview? What about the wounds the belief in separateness causes? What about basic goodness?

Grappling with systems change forces us to deal with the underlying thinking. It just doesn't help at this level to punish certain behaviors or shame people who aren't doing what we want. We can't force people to change their fundamental beliefs. What we *can* do is model the beliefs and values we want to see in the world and, in the process, create an environment of openness and respect where broader change through dialogue and relationship becomes possible.

It can help to ask ourselves, to ask our hearts: "What does the world most need right now"? If it's peace, love, and understanding; if it's nonviolence that pervades our thinking and our systems; if it's a world where the truth of interbeing is honored and acted upon; then it's important that that deep level of change be reflected in our activism and all areas of our lives. Consistent means and ends isn't a wimpy philosophy, it's a practical necessity.

Perhaps now, more than ever, we can appreciate the truth and urgency of the words of Dr. King, who, in his *I've Been to the Mountain Top* speech, delivered the day before he was assassinated, told us, "The choice is not between violence or nonviolence but between nonviolence or nonexistence."

Consistent nonviolence boils down to being conscious and mindful, to staying connected to our own bodies and emotional processes and working with what comes up. We stay with our vulnerability and longing and continue to cultivate self-acceptance. Consistent nonviolence is a practice, not a goal; a way of life, not a strategy.

> *I am but a weak aspirant, ever failing, ever trying. My failures make me more vigilant than before and intensify my faith. I can see with the eye of faith that the observance of the twin doctrine of truth and nonviolence has possibilities of which we have but very inadequate conception.*
> —Mahatma Gandhi, 1945[2]

Our spiritual essence aligns us with nonviolence. Nonviolence, in turn, aligns us with life and our spiritual essence. The world becomes richer and more beautiful, less black and white.

Obviously, keeping our activism in a spiritual context and staying the course with consistent nonviolence is not easy when there is so much pain and emotion that can hook us.

Putting our activism in the context of restoration helps us remember that all of our actions serve the ultimate purpose of cultivating our *own* maturity, of waking up and seeing through the illusion of separateness. It is only as a by-product of this that we become more effective agents for social change.

Practicing active peace has made it possible for me to hold consistent nonviolence as an intention, and this has changed who I am. I find myself becoming a stronger voice for the positive qualities and basic goodness of people who have done hurtful things and are not always easy to work with.

I'm much more able to resist the tendency to jump on the band-wagon of negativity and character assassination. I am more curious about people and why they do what they do. And yet, I still sometimes react in violent ways. I still get caught up in self-righteousness, insecurity, and shame and lash out at myself and others. I turn away and shut down. I forget all about interbeing. So continuing to come back to my intention is key. This leads me to continually remind myself that it's not about being perfect, and when I'm feeling stuck, to come back to self-awareness, to the body, to the breath; back to my resources, back to who I want to be.

This doesn't imply a joyless and never ending psychic and spiritual workout. I know I am in a process of healing and I need to cut myself some slack. I've started a light-hearted practice of naming the *shoulds*: When I catch myself thinking that something *should* be different, that something *should* not be happening, I just name that for myself with a sense of humor ("there I go again..."). When I bring consciousness and some lightness to what I'm thinking, and remember that the universe does not operate on the principle of should and should not, I immediately relax a little.

There *are* endless opportunities to practice being kind and giving priority to relationships, but making it a dreary chore doesn't serve transformation. I sometimes ask myself a basic question that keeps it simple: "Is my heart open right now?" If it is, compassion flows naturally. If it isn't, then there is something I can look at and explore—if I want to.

As I was finishing this book a dear friend sent me a tee shirt emblazoned on the front with the words: "I Sold Out to Westinghouse." It was one of several of those shirts I had made twenty years ago when I was campaigning against a hazardous waste incinerator Westinghouse was trying to build in Florida. I wanted to give the shirts to state legislators who refused to take action against the incinerator, and I wanted to do so in a dramatic way.

On the appointed day, when the issue was up for debate, security at the state capitol was on high alert, and friends told me upon my arrival that the capitol police were looking for me. I was so nervous that I was virtually out of my body but I managed to get by a few police officers and storm into the Senate chamber through the "members only" door. I interrupted their meeting to toss shirts at them and pull a life-size model of a human spine out of my backpack while I told them to "get a backbone."

I was quickly hauled out of the room—yelling vociferously all the way—and arrested. The belief that I was separate from those legislators was as vivid as it could possibly be. I wanted so much to make a difference and I can feel the self-righteousness and stress in my system as if it happened yesterday. I remember the feeling of isolation as I was being handcuffed. It wasn't the handcuffs and the prospect of jail, it was the longing to be connected and be heard that no amount of yelling was going to fill. Through my act of protest, I undermined myself on the most basic levels.

The friend who sent the shirts still believes that this direct action made an important contribution toward stopping the incinerator. I'm not so sure; I'm just glad I didn't create so much resentment that it was pushed through out of sheer spite. And when I think about how I rushed in there and started pulling things out of a backpack, I'm also glad I wasn't shot on the spot (fortunately, this was pre-9/11).

If I had been more able to keep my heart open, with restorative practices to support me back then, I would have done a lot of things very differently.

It is our spiritual essence and love of life that ultimately gives us the ability to stand up courageously to injustice. Connected to our wholeness, we move in a grounded and resilient way. We can hold people accountable for their actions and the harm they cause without shaming and blaming. We can seek to repair harm and change systems without seeking to punish people in the process. We can be with anger in honest and open ways that allow it to be transformed into healing energy. The path of active peace is a process, a practice imbued with awareness and love that ripples out to create more happiness and joy, and a more just and peaceful world.

Making peace is the most natural thing in the world once we begin to live into the truth of interbeing. A nonviolent world is an outgrowth of maturity, an essential and obvious aspect of our evolution as a species. Can we end all war forever? There's no way to know, but we can set our intention there and feel the aliveness that comes with that. Life longs for life. Life blesses us. The path of peace is a sacred path—the great work of our time. How wonderful it is to walk that path together!

Restorative Practice
Integration

For the final exercise in this book we turn toward integration. A lot of information has been presented, and practicing and integrating it all will take time. I hope this exercise will send you off in the best way possible.

Start once again with mindfulness. Connect with your breath and relax into your body.

When you are ready, reflect on what reading this book has left you with.

What feelings are present?

What thoughts are present?

How will you use what you have taken away from reading this book? Is there a specific intention in going forward from here that arises?

What restorative practices will you turn to for support?

What other kinds of support do you need? Are there specific people or groups that come to mind?

Then, dropping any sense of effort, take a moment and just feel how good it is to be alive right now.

Notice how, right in this very moment, when no thoughts interfere, everything just is what it is. Feel the perfection in that. Feel the relaxation.

Feel the support of the Earth and notice the beauty and blessings all around you.

How would it be, to trust in the sacred unfolding as you go forth, fully aware of your wholeness, spiritual essence, and the deep truth of interbeing?

Acknowledgements

A key turning point in the journey that led to the writing of this book was the Integral Peacemaker Training in Boulder, Colorado. Thank you Fleet Maull and Judith Ansara for masterminding and facilitating that eye- and heart-opening experience. Thank you Fleet for the no-nonsense introduction to meditation, and for providing opportunities for myself and many others to teach meditation in jails and prisons.

I offer the warmest of thanks to my restorative justice mentors, Beverley Title, Deb Witzel, Leslie Maya Charles, and the rest of the team in Colorado. I really had no idea what I was in for and how personally transformative restorative justice would be. It feels good to be a part of the movement and its merry band of practitioners.

To my teachers at Naropa University: John Davis, Jed Swift, Sherry Elms, Nancy Jane, Tina Fields, and the rest of the Transpersonal Psychology/Ecopsychology faculty—deep bows to you all. You and your program bring sanity to the world and nobody gets out unchanged. Bows to my classmates as well, you know who you are. You showed me what happens when heart, mind, spirit, and the fertile Earth get together and mix it up. The threads of connection go on and on.

I was blessed to have been a student to two of the finest Hakomi psychotherapy trainers imaginable, Melissa Grace and Phil Del Prince. Thank you for such a beautiful introduction into the workings of the human soul.

Thanks to Robert Gonzales with the Center for Living Compassion and my fellow students in the Life Program for the integration and transformation that has come through our compassion workouts.

Friends who came along for the ride and offered support and feedback include Eleanor Crow, John Ehrhart, James Churches, Charlie Cray, Roger Briggs, Sandy Shea, Steve Jones, Chuck Hancock, Don Greenfield, Alison Squier, Doug Dupler, Dale Greenawald, Patricia Hopkins, Steve Melville, Terri Melville, Stephen Bross, Kimberly Braun, and Lyna Norberg.

Special thanks to my mother, Stephanie Brown, for her unwavering optimism and love; and my father, Bill Brown, for his love and the crucial ways he and his parents made this work possible.

I offer deep gratitude to Samhitta Jones for her love and support, and for modeling integrity and self-connection in such an inspiring way.

This book was initiated seemingly out of the blue one day by a phone call from Andrew Harvey. Thank you Andrew for your emphatic prompting that day and your passionate example. Thanks also to Carolyn Baker for the early encouragement and the ongoing support.

And finally, thanks to Vera Wallen for her tireless edits from the cover to the last comma, and to Cheryl Genet, Managing Editor of the Collins Foundation Press, for her labor of love—including the many wise editorial suggestions—and for believing in me and my work.

Notes

Introduction and Chapter One

1. Rupert Ross, *Returning to the Teachings: Exploring Aboriginal Justice.* Toronto: Penguin Canada, 2006.

2. Ibid.

3. Maria Gimbutas, *The Language of the Goddess.* New York: Thames & Hudson, 2001.

4. Paul Shepard, *Nature and Madness.* Athens, GA: University of Georgia Press, 1982, 21–28.

5. Roger P. Briggs, *Journey to Civilization: The Science of How We Got Here.* Santa Margarita, CA: Collins Foundation Press, 2013.

6. Books pertaining to the Gnostic Gospels are great resources for reframing the life and teachings of Jesus in a life-affirming way. One book that has meant a lot to me is by the spiritual teacher Adyashanti. Adyashanti, *Resurrecting Jesus: Embodying the Spirit of a Revolutionary Mystic.* Boulder, CO: Sounds True, 2014.

7. Helen Ellerbe, *The Dark Side of Christian History.* Windermere, FL: Morningstar and Lark, 1995, 115–116.

8. Maria Gimbutas, *The Language of the Goddess.* New York: Thames & Hudson, 2001, 319.

9. See Bill Plotkin, *Nature and the Human Soul: Cultivating Wholeness and Community in a Fragmented World.* Novato, CA: New World Library, 2008; Andy Fisher, *Radical Ecopsychology: Psychology in the Service of Life.* Albany, NY: State University of New York Press, 2002; and Sarah Conn, Living in the Earth: Ecopsychology, Health and Psychotherapy. *The Humanistic Psychologist, 26(1–3)*, 1998, 179–198.

10. Sherry W. Nicholsen, *The Love of Nature and the End of the World: The Unspoken Dimensions of Environmental Concern.* Cambridge, MA: MIT Press, 2003, 148.

11. Marilyn M. Schlitz, et al. *Living Deeply: The Art and Science of Transformation in Everyday Life.* Oakland, CA: New Harbinger Publications, 2007, 8.

12. Aldous Huxley, "The Perennial Philosophy," In *Paths Beyond Ego: The Transpersonal Vision,* edited by Roger Walsh and Francis Vaughan. Los Angeles: Tarcher/Perigree, 1993, 212–213.

13. Deepak Chopra, *The Love Poems of Rumi.* New York: Harmony Books, 1998, p. 44.

14. Margaret Wheatley, *Leadership and the New Science: Discovering Order in a Chaotic World.* San Francisco: Berrett-Koehler Publishers, 2006, 34.

Chapter Two

1. The World Bank, *Turn Down the Heat: Why a 4° Warmer World Must be Avoided,* November 18, 2012. The report can be downloaded for free at http://www.worldbank.org.

2. The World Bank, Executive Summary, *Turn Down the Heat: Why a 4° Warmer World Must be Avoided,* November 18, 2012, xviii. Available at http://www.worldbank.org.

3. See *The Living Planet Report 2014: Species and spaces, people and places,* World Wildlife Fund; http://wwf.panda.org

4. See Juliette Jowit, "Humans driving extinction faster than species can evolve, say experts." The Guardian, March 7, 2010; http://www.guardian.co.uk/environment/2010/mar/07/extinction-species-evolve; and John Vidal, "Protect nature for world economic security, warns UN biodiversity chief." *The Guardian,* August 16, 2010; http://www.guardian.co.uk/environment/2010/aug/16/nature-economic-security.

5. In Gary Snyder, *A Place in Space: Ethics, Aesthetics, and Watersheds.* New York: Counterpoint, 1995, 137.

6. Democracy Now!, "Chilean Economist Manfred Max-Neef on Barefoot Economics, Poverty and Why the U.S. is Becoming an 'Underdeveloping Nation'." November 26, 2011; http://www.democracynow.org/2010/11/26/chilean_economist_manfred_max_neef_on.

7. Lao-Tzu, *Tao Te Ching*, translated by Stephen Mitchell. New York: Harper & Row, 1988, 77.

Chapter Three

1. Carolyn Baker, *Sacred Demise: Walking the Spiritual Path of Industrial Civilization's Collapse.* Bloomington, IN: IUniverse, 2009, 24.

Chapter Four

1. Victor E. Frankl, *Man's Search for Meaning: An Introduction to Logotherapy.* New York: Simon & Schuster, 1984, 75.

2. Daniel Goleman, *Emotional Intelligence: Why It Can Matter More than IQ.* New York: Bantam, 2006, xv.

3. Shunryu Suzuki, *Zen Mind, Beginner's Mind: Informal Talks on Zen Meditation and Practice.* New York: Weatherhill, 1998, 111.

4. The poem is called, "Call Me by My True Names," and it can be found in Thich Nhat Hanh's book, *Peace is Every Step: The Path of Mindfulness in Everyday Life.* New York: Bantam, 1992, 123–124. If I had but one book to recommend to the peacemaker, it would be this one.

Chapter Five

1. Paul Shepard, *Thinking Animals: Animals and the Development of Human Intelligence.* New York: Viking Press, 1978, 29.

2. See Sharon Salzberg, *Real Happiness: The Power of Meditation*. New York: Workman Publishing, 2011; and Daniel J. Siegel, *The Mindful Brain: Reflection and Attunement in the Cultivation of Well-being*. New York: W. W. Norton, 2007.

3. See Sharon Salzberg, *Real Happiness: The Power of Meditation*. New York: Workman Publishing, 2011; and Bob Stahl and Elisha Goldstein, *A Mindfulness-Based Stress Reduction Workbook*. Oakland, CA: New Harbinger, 2010.

4. Chögyam Trungpa, *Shambhala: The Sacred Path of the Warrior*. Boston: Shambhala, 1984. 29–33.

Chapter Six

1. See Ronald Wright, *A Short History of Progress*. New York: Carroll & Graf Publishers, 2005, 32; and Paul Shepard, *The Tender Carnivore and the Sacred Game*. Athens, GA: University of Georgia Press, 1973.

2. Thanks to the faculty of Naropa University's Transpersonal Psychology/Ecopsychology program for introducing me to this exercise.

3. See Richard Louv, *The Nature Principle: Human Restoration and the End of Nature-Deficit Disorder*. Chapel Hill, NC: Algonquin Books, 2011; Bill Plotkin, *Nature and the Human Soul: Cultivating Wholeness and Community in a Fragmented World*. Novato, CA: New World Library, 2008; Sarah Conn, Living in the Earth: Ecopsychology, Health and Psychotherapy. *The Humanistic Psychologist, 26(1–3)*, 1998, 179–198; and Andy Fisher, *Radical Ecopsychology: Psychology in the Service of Life*. Albany, NY: State University of New York Press, 2002.

4. Sarah Conn, Living in the Earth: Ecopsychology, Health and Psychotherapy. *The Humanistic Psychologist, 26(1–3)*, 1998, 183–184.

5. Jeannette Armstrong, "Keepers of the Earth," in *Ecopsychology: Restoring the Earth, Healing the Mind,* edited by Theodore Roszak, Mary E. Gomes, and Allen D. Kanner, 1995, 320–321. San Francisco: Sierra Club Books.

6. Mark Coleman, *Awake in the Wild: Mindfulness in Nature as a Path of Self-Discovery.* Makawao, Maui, HI: Inner Ocean Publishing, 2006.

7. Simon Blackburn, *Ethics: A Very Short Introduction.* New York: Oxford University Press, 2001.

8. Kenny Ausubel, *Restoring the Earth: Visionary Solutions from the Bioneers.* Tiburon, CA: H J Kramer, 1997.

9. Aldo Leopold, *A Sand County Almanac.* New York: Ballantine Books, 1978, 262.

10. See Richard Louv, *The Nature Principle: Human Restoration and the End of Nature-Deficit Disorder.* Chapel Hill, NC: Algonquin Books, 2011; and Craig Chalquist, "Bibliography of Ecotherapy Research," in *Ecotherapy: Healing with Nature in Mind,* edited by Linda Buzzell and Craig Chalquist. San Francisco: Sierra Club Books, 2009, 296–305.

11. Victor E. Frankl, *Man's Search for Meaning: An Introduction to Logotherapy.* New York: Simon & Schuster, 1984, 78.

Chapters Seven

1. John Seed, Joanna Macy, Pat Fleming, and Arne Naess, *Thinking Like a Mountain: Toward a Council of All Beings.* Philadelphia: New Society Publishers, 1988, 36.

2. The International Crane Foundation states that a fossil found in Nebraska, estimated to be approximately ten million years old, was of a bird "structurally identical" to the modern sandhill crane, thus making the sandhill one of the oldest surviving bird species; https://www.savingcranes.org/sandhill-crane.

(No references in Chapter Eight)

Chapter Nine

1. Marshall Rosenberg, *Nonviolent Communication: A Language of Life*. Encinitas, CA: PuddleDancer Press, 2003, 52–53.

2. Marshal Rosenberg's pioneering work in Nonviolent Communication has done much to bring the importance of feelings and needs into popular culture. Comprehensive lists of feelings and needs, along with many other resources can found at The Center for Nonviolent Communication's website; www.cnvc.org.

3. Thanks to Robert Gonzales with The Center for Living Compassion for inspiring this exercise; www.living-compassion.org.

4. Thanks to Judith Ansara and Robert Gass with Sacred Union for providing the basis for this list; www.sacredunion.com.

5. Thanks to Fleet Maull and Kate Crisp for their teachings on the Drama Triangle; www.prisonmindfulness.org.

6. Thich Nhat Hanh, *Interbeing: Fourteen Guidelines for Engaged Buddhism*. Berkeley, CA: Parallax Press, 1998, 42.

7. Marshall Rosenberg, *Nonviolent Communication: A Language of Life*. Encinitas, CA: PuddleDancer Press, 2003.

Chapter Ten

1. There are many resources available for learning more about restorative justice. Howard Zehr's, *The Little Book of Restorative Justice*, and *The Little Book of Restorative Discipline for Schools* by Lorraine Amstutz and Judy Mullet provide good introductions. I can also recommend *Teaching Peace: A Restorative Justice Framework for Strengthening Relationships*, a book by one of my mentors, Beverly Title. Rupert Ross's *Returning to the Teachings* is important for helping us understand the deep roots of restorative justice and the holistic direction in which it might continue to evolve.

2. I refer readers to experts on this subject such as Diana and Michael Richardson whose work I highly recommend; www.loveforcouples.com.

3. This is another exercise inspired by Robert Gonzales with The Center for Living Compassion; www.living-compassion.org.

Chapter Eleven

1. Thanks to Robert Gonzales with The Center for Living Compassion for his teachings on true mourning; www.living-compassion.org.

2. Street retreats are a specialty of the Zen Peacemakers; more information at http://zenpeacemakers.org/events/street-retreats/.

3. Abraham H. Maslow, *The Farther Reaches of Human Nature.* New York: Viking, 1971, 43.

4. Malte Klar and Tim Kasser, "Some Benefits of Being an Activist: Measuring Activism and its Role in Psychological Well-Being," *Political Psychology, Vol. 30, Issue 5,* October 2009, 755–777.

Chapter Twelve

1. That letter and some related posts can be found on my blog at www.4activepeace.com

2. Mahatma Gandhi, *All Men are Brothers: Autobiographical Reflections.* New York: Continuum, 2005, 92.

Index

About the Author

Scott Brown is a visionary peacemaker who bridges the divides between psychology and spirituality, the personal and the political, mindfulness and activism. He is a leading advocate for bringing the principles and practices of restorative justice to bear on the full range of social issues and transforming activism into peacemaking. He is a life and relationship coach, youth mentor, and trainer who has applied his skills as a restorative justice facilitator and program coordinator, a divorce mediator, a wilderness rites of passage guide, a meditation instructor, and as a mentor to youth both in and out of the criminal justice system.

Scott worked for over 15 years on the front lines of environmental activism as a campaigner with organizations including Greenpeace, the Idaho Conservation League, and the Canadian Parks and Wilderness Society.

Scott holds a Master's degree in Ecopsychology and Transpersonal Psychology from Naropa University, and is the founder of Active Peace, LLC, and cofounder of the Colorado Center For Restorative Practices. He is co-host of the Restoration Dialogues podcast, and lives in Boulder, Colorado.

Join the Active Peace Facebook group – www.facebook.com/groups/activepeace

www.4ActivePeace.com

Other books from the
Collins Foundation Press
More information and purchase available at
www.CollinsFoundationPress.org

Becoming Intimate with the Earth invites you to embrace the blessing as well as the shadow of modern culture. It seamlessly weaves together our new science-based cosmology, the traitional wisdom of indegenous people, and an artist's passionate engagement with life.

Pauline Le Bel is a masterful storyteller, award-winning novelist, and Emmy-nominated screenwriter who integrates music, science, nature, and spirit for the benefit of the entire Earth Family.

Journey to Civilization: The Science of How We Got Here reveals a new story based on the evidence and skepticism of science. It explores and explains the science itself, from the physics of stars and the formation of rocky planets, to the evolution of life and the epic journey of humans out of Africa to become the rulers of the Earth.

Roger Briggs is retired from a thirty-year career as an acclaimed high school physics teacher and educational science writer.

CPSIA information can be obtained
at www.ICGtesting.com
Printed in the USA
FFOW01n1356070317
33192FF

9 780988 438293